PERSUASION TECHNIQUES:

How to Stop Being Manipulated. Learn the Method and The Secrets of Manipulation and Persuasion. How To Influence People With Mind Control techniques.

TABLE OF CONTENTS

INTRODUCTION

Consider your audience in phrasing your message. The way you address college students must be different from the way you address senior citizens. You may also have to modify the different genders.

Let us use the example of health products once again; weight loss products to be precise. When introducing such products to women, you can emphasize the need to look good in cute dresses, avoid stretch marks, acquire a bikini body and so on. These are issues that are close to their hearts.

Men may not respond as effectively to a message phrased as such. The word 'fat' seems not to sound as atrocious to men as it does to women. If the old clothes don't fit, how about just get others a size (or 3) larger? And don't even get started about the beach. They'll comfortably spot their beer bellies, shirtless, and enjoy their holiday without a care in the world. They insert 'big' before their name and actually make it sound cool. Thank you very much, Big Austin.

See? A message that was well-received by the women goes in and out for the men. Perhaps the way to get men to listen in this case would be to hit below the belt, quite literally. Tie your products to sexual health. Sexual prowess, to be exact. The idea that they can be beasts (or close) in bed can get them eating oats and celery sticks in no time. Or whatever else you suggest.

If you're speaking to a creative, such as an artist, do not drown them in analytical figures. Spare that for the business executives. These ones are fascinated by numbers, they say they don't lie. Creatives thrive in hearing how ideas will come to life.

You must carefully choose which detail to exemplify depending on whom you're speaking to. These are just a few examples of personalizing the message depending on the receiver. The principal goes beyond the business world to other facets of life. You should now be in a position to do the same depending on your situation.

When people do not positively receive your message right away, you have to be prepared to say it time and again. Sounds like nagging, right? Not necessarily. Think of politicians campaigning for political posts.

They campaign for months, speaking to people every day, essentially repeating the same message over and over. Should they lose that particular election, they return the following one and continue expounding the reasons they believe they're best placed to represent the people. Former President Abraham Lincoln lost 8 separate elections before he was elected to the highest office in the land.

There is something about a man (or woman) who asks without ceasing. One who refuses to back down. The persistence convinces people that he has ideas that will make an impact on their lives. Even the most stubborn of them end up listening.

How can you remain persistent without being a nuisance? Keep paraphrasing the message. Say things differently. Add some more details each time. Develop a demo or prototype. Collect relevant statistics. People respond better to something they can see as opposed to plain words. Give the listeners time to process the information, then communicate again. Keep knocking on that door, and eventually, it'll be opened one way or the other.

To make others see your point of view, you have to communicate with conviction. Your verbal and body language makes the first impression and determines the perception of the listener towards you. Whether you're giving a speech, speaking to a small group of people or to a single person, confidence is key.

How do you portray confidence? Body language first. Walk with your head high. Maintain steady eye contact. Shake hands firmly. This will make people want to hear what you have to say. Listen attentively when it's the listeners turn to speak. Nod periodically.

Confidence carries an aura of energy that is instantly transferred to others. It motivates and excites them about your ideas. They can see that you're totally sold on the idea, and this will increase their curiosity and make them want to try it.

Make your listener see that there is a limited time. This is a strategy mostly used in marketing. What do they tell you? Hurry while stocks last! Offer valid for the first 100 buyers! Buy today and get a discount! In most of these sales, the stock is not limited as they want to make you believe. They know a sense of urgency works. They manage to convince you that it'll be a privilege to be among the first buyers and receive a certain offer. And it works.

Still, on marketing matters, make sure you demonstrate that other people have shown interest or given good reviews of your ideas. In this age of social media, you can rely on the response that you're getting online as proof of interest.

Begin by posting your idea online on multiple platforms. You can sponsor an advert in which you're in a position to so that more people can view it. As is the case with interesting ideas, it goes viral. Scores of people will view your pictures, watch your videos or read the articles. Even better, they share the content and just like that; it's exposed to a larger audience. Fortunately, social media platforms keep track of it all. Numbers sure don't lie. Use those hits, likes, shares, follows and comments in your next pitch. People are drawn to ideas that have fascinated other people. They don't want to be left behind, they want to be part of the excitement too.

WHAT IS PERSUASION?

When we discuss manipulation and persuasion, it usually comes down to a difference of intent. For instance, is the person who is persuading you to do something that will benefit both you and them? If so, that's the classic win-win scenario, and we could say that persuasion was used to help you come to the right decision.

But what if the same person gets you to do something that benefits him, but leaves you worse off? That would be characterized as manipulation, and that type of persuasion happens all of the time, too. You may have done it yourself without really realizing it, and not felt too good about it afterward.

Persuasion can be used for all kinds of purposes, both good and evil. People can manipulate you into giving them your money, your time, your faith, your talent, and provide you with nothing in return. Or they can persuade you into giving of all of these things and leave you better off in the end. And sometimes, the lines aren't so clearly drawn.

What I will attempt to show you in this book is just how persuasion happens in various parts of your everyday life, how persuasion can be used to help you get what you want, and how to recognize persuasion techniques that are used on you. Ultimately, everyone makes their own decisions. By being aware of persuasion techniques, you can more successfully analyze your motivations and make sure that what you are doing benefits both you and others.

Today's Pervasive Persuasion

Persuasion is also an important topic today because we are contacted by more and more sophisticated methods of persuasion than ever before. Persuasion comes at us in all forms, at a velocity never even possible previously. I'm sure you can guess the cause of this increased persuasion. That's right! It's called The Internet.

Never before have people had direct access to the tools of mass communication. You can pick up your smartphone and start broadcasting live right now, with just a few clicks. You can start typing and send your views to millions of people around the world. Or you can post a picture of that adorable thing your cat just did to your partner to brighten their day at work. And all of the people you are reaching can get that information instantly because they probably have a smartphone or computer or screen nearby that they are looking at, and you have access to that network. This type of reach and access was unheard of only a decade or two ago. Today, this connection is commonplace and growing.

But do you ever take time to decide how the words and pictures that you consume play a part in what you think, or what the motives were behind sending them to you in the first place? Much like a loaded gun in the hands of someone who doesn't know how to shoot, persuasion techniques can sometimes have unintended consequences that can be devastating. If you don't realize what the warning signs are, or how you can protect yourself from those consequences, and make sure you aren't unintentionally harming yourself.

The Principles of Persuasion

Since that book, many researchers have created experiments to test these theories with surprisingly consistent results. The bottom line is that we humans seem to be hard-wired to behave in certain ways given certain circumstances. Using various methods to trigger those responses that we want, we can cause the outcomes that we want.

The 6 Principles of Persuasion

Reciprocation

Give something to get something, right? Remember the story of the chicken who planted grain so that her chicks could eat? She asked for help to sow the grain, to keep the field clean from weeds, to harvest the grain and finally, to make the bread. She asked her neighbors and friends to help, but in the end, no one was interested until the bread was hot and ready to eat. Since her neighbors had not given her anything in the form of help, she was not inclined to give them any of the final product.

That give and take is the first principal of getting along in life, and it's known as one of the foundational principals of persuasion as well. Reciprocity merely means that if you give someone something, they are more likely to give you something in return.

Commitment and Consistency

We, humans, have a "reality" surrounding us at all times. I put this "reality" in quotes because it is a reality of our creation.

Our brains have an innate ability to tell stories, and we tell ourselves stories all of the time. We tell ourselves stories of the type of person we believe we are, and how we behave feeds into that story. When presented with a choice, you make that choice based on the story of who you are. One of the options looks "right" to us because making that choice is consistent with what we believe a person like us would do.

Social Proof

This core persuasion principle is also sometimes referred to as Consensus. Social proof feeds directly from the previous storytelling of Commitment and Consistency. We have told ourselves a story of what we believe we are, what we stand for, and the kind of person we are. To reinforce that story, we look at how other people behave for Social Proof of how people like us should react in a particular situation.

Now more than ever, the Internet has created countless places where we can go for this type of reinforcement. Some of that reinforcement is legitimate, some not so much. All of it is used as a powerful tool for persuasion, as we'll find out going forward.

Authority

Now once we have decided on the type of person we are and we've assembled with the kinds of people we believe reinforce that identity; the next step is to seek out knowledgeable people to reinforce what we've told ourselves to be true. That's where the idea of Authority takes hold.

As sane people, we are likely to take the advice of people who appear to have more knowledge about a subject than we do. That is certainly necessary. No one can know everything, not even with smartphones and Google just a tap away. We seek out the advice of people who know more about a subject than we do. We'll talk more about using this in persuasion later.

Liking

Liking is one of those core principles that seems obvious, but yet it needs definition since it is at the hub of all types of persuasion. Liking, simply put, means that you are much more likely to be persuaded by someone that you like.

If you don't like someone, are you going to take their advice? Probably not. We humans are wired to make snap judgments about almost every situation we get into, and one of the simplest decisions to make is whether we like someone or not. Every person you meet triggers a feeling instantly of comfort or wariness. This was a survival skill in the early days of our evolution, and it still holds sway today, as we'll see.

Scarcity

Speaking of evolution's early days, our final persuasion principal is an obvious holdover from the early days of staying alive. Scarcity makes things more valuable to us, so when something seems like it is limited in quantity, we are more likely to want it.

Sand is commonplace; gold is not. Which would you rather have? Or more to the point, what does all humankind want more? It most certainly used to be food that was so valuable, so that early man found ways to preserve food when it was abundant so that it would be around when food got scarce.

Survival depends on specific resources that can be in short supply, so humans are naturally prone to try and save and hang on to that which is not always available. Since this is core hardwiring in our brains, we'll see that this is an often-used method of persuasion today.

METHODS OF PERSUASION

For some people, the art of persuasion comes easily. You can watch them talk to almost anyone, and it seems like they will always get the response that they want from the other person. On the other hand, there are those people who may have the best message in the world who couldn't convince anyone, even their closest friends, to do something. No matter where you fall in either of these groups though, with a little bit of practice and hard work, you will be able to learn how to use persuasion to your advantage.

In terms of the process of using persuasion, there will usually be three parts that you need to follow including:

The communicator, or the medium used as the source of persuasion

The persuasive nature of the appeal

The audience or the target person that the appeal is going to be sent too.

Each of these elements needs to be accounted for before you try to use persuasion on a higher level. It is always a good practice to look around you and check to see how many instances of persuasion are going on in your daily life. Some of these are going to be overt, but many of them are going to be pretty subtle. This can be great training for persuasion because you will be able to employ the same kind of tactics. Let's take a look at some of the options that you can use when it comes to good persuasion and using the right techniques.

Using the Aristotelian appeals

So, the first option that we are going to look at is the Aristotelian appeals. Aristotle is well-known and is actually one of the most famous persuaders of all time. He believed that there were three main ways that a person could approach thing when they were trying to use persuasion to change the opinion of the other person.

Ethos

The first appeal that one could use was ethos, which is going to focus on things such as trust, integrity, and character. This appeal is going to focus on the reputation of the person and some of the things that they may have done in the past, or even how others think about them today. There are many people who value their reputations, and they will work hard to maintain them, especially if the person is in a high office or in the public eye. This is not a bad thing to care about your reputation.

As the persuader, it is fine to show off some character because this shows that you are a human like everyone else and you can even show off some of the flaws that you have. The trick here is that you need to only show off flaws that are pretty small, ones that the target audience will not see as a big deal, but they do need to be large enough that they show that you are still a person who has some good values and even virtues.

You need to be credible as well if you would like to be persuasive. People are much more likely to believe what you are saying if you are seen as a credible person, someone who is seen as an expert in their chosen field. If you would like to get started with persuading other people to act in a specific way, then you need to start cultivating the right impression with good virtues, small flaws, and by showing that you are an expert in your field.

Pathos

The second appeal that you should work on is pathos, which is when you evoke the emotions of the other person. You will want to find some way to excise the other person, to get their interest in some way. This can often be done with storytelling or even by referencing situations where injustices were done at some point. You can add in some ethos to this by condemning these actions and describing how your values fall into the matter.

If you are working on this appeal, it is important to use the right linguistics. Language is going to be your most important tool for getting the emotions involved. A good speaker will always be able to pick out the right words to get their message out there. For example, they know how to use words that will amplify or subdue the situation based on the results that you want to get.

This can be hard to learn in the beginning, especially if

you do not consider yourself to be that great of a speaker. But the next time that there is a big pollical debate or speech going on take the time to listen to the words that they are using. This will help you to see how the words can bring out the right emotions that the communicator is looking for.

Logos

And the third appeal that you can use when it comes to persuasion is logos. This is when you are going to use logic, rational explanations, and even evidence to help support your claims. Some people do not respond that well to the emotional side, and they may feel that anyone who is using their values and integrity are only doing so to make a sale. These people are probably going to do the best with logos, being told logical information that they can look up on their own to verify before they make a decision.

This does not mean that you cannot go through and make some changes to the wording and try to convince these people still. You can always bring the most prominent features to light, or if you know the person, at least bring out the features that are going to appeal to them the most. This is not a license to lie to them about the things that you are doing and saying, but it doesn't hurt to show your argument in the best possible light.

Foot in the door

We talked about this one a bit earlier, but it can be one of the most effective persuasion techniques that are out there. This one allows you to ask for a bigger favor after you have already been granted a smaller favor, especially if they are related in some way. You may start off with something that is pretty small, such as just borrowing a cup of sugar from your neighbor. Your neighbor will probably be fine with this because it's not that big of a deal and most people, as long as they have it on hand, will have a cup of sugar to share with you.

Now that you have asked for that cup of sugar, you may take it up a notch. You may then ask if they have some butter and eggs that you can borrow as well. Since they have already lent you some sugar, they figure it is not a big deal to lend you some more things a well. And the persuader can just keep going, perhaps asking if the target would mind baking the whole cake for them in the end.

If the persuader had started out with asking the neighbor to make the cake, it is unlikely that the neighbor would have agreed. The neighbor might say that they are busy or that they really do not know how to make a cake that well. But since the persuader started out with something small, something that would be silly not to help out with, and then slowly built up from there, the neighbor may eventually feel a sense of obligation to get the work done at this point.

This method can be used in many different persuasion circumstances. The trick is to always start out with something small, something that you think the target will be willing to help you out with. Then you will slowly build yourself up until you get to the bigger thing that you would like them to have in the long run. You may have wanted the target to start with the bigger thing, but if you went there first, you would have completely missed out on the sale.

Reversal tagging

Another option that you can use is known as reversal tagging. This is a trick that uses simple and subtle sentence phrasing to get an agreement, or at least compliance, from the target in general. It is going to use two opposing structures inside the sentence, the first part being an affirmative statement and the second one will be a tag question.

The premise here is that you will make the initial statement to open the line of questioning, but you will add on the tag question so that the target has a binary choice for answering. This will help you to reframe the response so that it sounds like they agree with you the whole time.

For example, you may say something like "You like this house, don't you?" to your spouse. There are a few ways that they can choose to respond to this. If they say "Yes, I like this place" you would respond something like "As I thought, you like this place." On the other hand, if they give you a different response, such as "No, I don't like this place," you can simply turn it around and say "As I thought, you don't like this place."

Statements like the one above are designed to have a negative reversal element to them. If you do them in the proper manner, the statement will hide the command because it becomes a rhetorical question because it will first tell the person what they should be thinking, but then it inserts the question that will offer a level of disagreement, even though it implies that the disagreement is not wanted.

The key to this method is to ensure that the first statement is pretty strong because it is going to be the main persuasive component. This kind of technique is also useful when you are trying to convince the other person to take an action on something, rather than just agreeing with you. It is the same principle, but this time you will state out your negative first before taking a long pause and then adding in the tag question. For example, you could say something like "You aren't able to do that…. Are you?" this implies that the person is not able to do something and it is going to evoke them to respond in a way that will prove you wrong.

Reverse psychology

This is something that you have probably heard about in the past because it is a psychological tactic that is often used when you want to get the other person to take an action. However, if you are not good at performing this tactic, it is going to seem pretty obvious, and it will not work the way that you would like it to. This tactic is basically going to get somebody to do what you would like by suggesting that they do the opposite in the beginning. It is going to be the most effective if you can evoke an emotional response because it will stop the person from thinking rationally through their decision.

This is a principle that can work well with those who like to have control, such as rebellious people or those who just like to do the opposite of what they are told to do. It is often called reactance theory, and it will describe the scenario where a person feels like they are losing control of things and they are going to try to grab that control back by doing the exact opposite of what they have been asked, even if it is not their best interest to do so.

Cognitive dissonance

Have you ever been in a situation where you know that something seems a bit off about it, but you cannot figure out why it doesn't feel right? When there isn't something quite right about a situation, it is going o set off some dissonance in the mind and will trigger the person to try to make it all right. People who have OCD will often know this feeling because they will notice when little things are out of the normal.

If you can change things up a little bit, you may be able to convince the other person to act in the way that you would like. They may feel that their reputation is falling a little bit, that they are missing out on something, or so much else. You can then step in to offer them a solution, an easy to way to change things back to normal, and they are more likely to jump right at it.

Counter-attitudinal advocacy

It is pretty common for people to state a view on something, or even to support an opinion, even if that is not something that they really believe themselves. This isn't necessarily that deceptive because the things that people choose to do this with are usually small or they have the best intentions. For example, it is common for someone to tell a little white lie because it will help to protect the feelings of someone else. When this happens, we are attempting to reduce the dissonance that we caused by saying that our actions are still noble.

Whether you think that telling a little white lie or doing something similar is acceptable or that you think honesty is the best option is irrelevant because you can still use this human tendency to your advantage when you are persuading others. This is a common technique to use when it comes to cults or even gangs when they are trying to change the beliefs of others to justify their behavior.

When you are using this as a persuasion principle, you are going to be tied in with what is known as incremental escalating requests. What this one means is that you are going to offer the target with some small rewards so that they are not really going to attribute this new behavior to some changes. Over time though, the effect is going to keep escalating until it reaches a point where they are doing something that is really different compared to where the behavior started.

A good way to practice this is by getting those you know to go along with you on some small points, but these small points need to have an eventual goal of persuasion that you would like to accomplish. These points need to all be small enough that the internal justification for agreeing with you is not that big of a deal and the other person is not going to resist you or have a lot of questions in the process. Over time, if you have done this properly, the beliefs of the other people should change to fit with yours.

Perceived self-interest

If you ask anyone, they often believe that they are generous and pretty caring creatures. No matter how much most people believe this though, as humans we are really a self-serving species. There have been a lot of studies done on this over the years, and it has been proven over and over again. Even altruism is a self-serving act because it does help the grantor to feel good about themselves in the process.

The idea behind this technique is a pretty simple one to work with, but you will be spending your time on perception. If you can convince your target that they are doing something that is in their best interest, whether that is true or not, then the target is much more likely to go along with the whole thing. This can be really apparent when you are trying to persuade someone who is higher up than you.

For example, you may work with your boss, and you can say something like "I see my job as making you more successful." This can help to endear a new employee to their boss because even if you are getting some of the credit along the way, you are showing that the majority of the limelight is going to go to your boss along the way, and their self-interest is really going to like this.

This one is known as disrupt-then-reframe, and it is similar to offer biasing and Russian front. The idea with this one is to put out a statement that is completely far away from the ideals and belief of the target right from the beginning. This is like making an offer to the other person that they are not really likely to accept. After they have rejected your offer, you are going to do a follow up that is more rational, something that your target is more likely to go along with, especially since they are still comparing it to your first offer in their heads. Of course, the second suggestion that you make is usually going to be the one that you wanted to persuade the target to in the first place.

It is similar to reverse tagging, but it is going to

include a longer statement. The aim here is to disrupt the other person is thinking and then show them that you can still be rational in the process and that you want to work with them to a better goal. Since you are working with them, and the second request is not so ridiculous compared to the first one that you made, the target is much more likely to go along with what you are suggesting.

Hurt and rescue principle

This principle is going to be based off evoking some discomfort or fear in the person from the start. When the person is assessing their options for a solution, you will be able to offer the perfect solution in the form of the thing you want to persuade them to. You need to be able to manufacture a level of discomfort here first and being crafty enough to make this work can be hard.

Since you are trying to bring in some fear or discomfort with your target, you do need to be a bit careful with this option. It is not a good idea to come off as aggressive or intimidating in the process because this will just turn the person away from you completely.

For example, you may work with someone and say that you have noticed that their performance has dropped off recently and that there may be an issue with their funding getting cut off because of it. Now that the other person is worried about what is going to happen with their funding and their job, you can come in as the one with a solution. You may say something like you have convinced them to not do that just yet as long as the other person can start meeting their performance metrics again.

Of course, you will need to go through and change things around to work with the thing that you are trying to sell or the thing that you are trying to persuade the other person to do. But the point is that you will start out by adding in some discomfort or fear for the target before providing them with the solution that will make things all better.

Trial ballooning

Another option that you can use is known as trial ballooning or trial closing. This is the starting point, and it is relevant whether you are the seller or the buyer in the negotiation. The idea is to start out with the final solution that you would like to end up. You will just put that information out there and see if the thing works.

With this tactic, there is nothing wrong with going a little bit big right from the beginning. Being the one to make the first offer in this kind of exchange will usually put you in the worst position because you have shown all of your cards and this is why it is so important for you to go as bold as possible. When you start out with an aggressive offer, it will provide the anchor that is needed to help you get a good deal. The other person is going to bring you down from that anchor spot so going high helps you to get closer to your goals.

And you never know, your big offer may not seem so bad to the other person, and they may be willing to just give in right from the beginning. If the other person is really in a hurry to come to a resolution, they will really take this balloon offer, and you will come out ahead.

Auction model

This strategy is a good one to put in place if you are working with more than one buyer at the same time.

Otherwise, it is not going to be the best one. With this method, you want to play one of the parties against the others so that there is a buying frenzy and it is more likely that the price is going to be driven up, no matter what you are trying to sell.

It is human nature to be competitive, and when they are faced with some opposition to something that they would like, their primitive instincts are going to come out. Possession seems to be an innate for most of us, especially if we haven't gone through to rationally appraise the real use for the item ahead of time. The persuader will be able to use their advantage, getting all the buyers in the deal to jump on board and try to pay more than the other person.

As you can see, there are a lot of different techniques that you can use when it comes to being successful with persuasion. The one that you will choose often depends on the goals that you have in mind, what you are trying to persuade the other person to do, your comfort level, and how hard the other person will be to persuade. Try a few of them out and see which one works the best for you.

HYPNOSIS

What Is Hypnosis

There have been many definitions about what hypnosis actually is. Hypnosis has been defined by the American Psychological Association as a cooperative interaction where the hypnotist will give suggestions to the person, he picks which he or she will respond to. Edmonton said that a person is simply but in a deep state of mind when in undergoing hypnosis. Hypnosis is therefore when a person enters a state of mind in which a person finds himself or herself vulnerable to the suggestions of a hypnotist. Hypnosis is not new to us because many people have seen it in movies, cartoons or actually been to magic shows or performances where participants are told to do usual acts and they do it. One thing is for sure that, some people do believe that hypnosis actually exist and would do anything to avoid being a victim while others believe that its fiction.

Induction

Induction is considered as stage one of hypnosis. There are three stages in total. Induction is aimed at intensifying the partaker's expectations of what follows after, explaining the role they will be playing, seeking their attention and any other steps needed during this stage. There are many methods used by hypnotists to induce a participant to hypnosis. One of them is the "Braidism" technique which requires a hypnotist to follow a few steps. This technique is named after James Braid. First step would be to begin with finding a bright object and hold it in your left hand and specifically between the middle, fore, and thumb fingers. The object should be placed where the participant will be able to fix his or her stare and maintain the stare. This position would be the above the forehead. It is always important that the hypnotist remind the partaker to keep his or her eyes on the object. If the participant wonders away from the object, the process will not work. The participant should be completely focused on the object. The participant's eyes will begin to dilate and the participant will begin to have a wavy motion. A hypnotist will know that his participant is in a trance when the participant involuntarily closes his or her eyelids when the middle and fore fingers of the right hand are carried from the eyes to the object. When this does not happen, the participant is begins again being guided that their eyes are to close when the fingers are used in a similar motion. Where therefore, this puts the participant in an altered state of mind he or she is said to be hypnotized. The induction technique has been considered not to be necessary for every case and research has shown that this stage is not as important as previously had been known when it came to the effects of induction technique. Over the years, there have been variations in the once original hypnotic induction technique while others have preferred to use other alternatives. James Braid innovation of this technique still stands out.

Suggestion

After Induction, the next stage that follows is the suggestion stage. James Braid left out the word suggestion when he first defined hypnosis. He however described this stage as attempting to draw the conscious mind of the partaker to focus on one central idea. James Braid would start by minimising the functions of different parts of the partaker's body. He would then put more emphasis on the use of verbal and non-verbal suggestions to begin to get the partaker into a hypnotic state. Hippolyte Bernheim also shifted from the physical state of the partaker. This well-known hypnotist described hypnosis as the induction of a peculiar physical condition which increases ones susceptibility to the suggestions by the participant. Suggestions can be verbal or one that doesn't involve speech. Modern hypnotist uses different form of suggestions that include non-verbal cues, direct verbal suggestions, metaphors and insinuations. Non-verbal suggestions that may be used include changing the tone, mental imagery and physical manipulation. Mental imagery can take two forms. One includes those that are delivered with permission and those that are done none the less and are more authoritarian.

When discussing hypnosis, it would be wise if one would be able to distinguish between the conscious mind and unconscious mind. Most hypnosis while using suggestions will try and trigger the conscious mind other than the unconscious mind. While other hypnotists will view it as way of communicating with the unconscious mind. Hypnotists such as Hippolyte Bernheim and James Braid together with other great hypnotists see it as trying to communicate with the conscious mind. This is what they believed. James Braid even defines hypnosis as the attention that is focused upon the suggestion. The idea that a hypnotist will be able to encroach into your unconscious mind and order you around is next to impossible as according to those who belong to Braids school of thought. The determinant of the different conceptions about suggestions has also been the nature of the mind. Hypnotists such as Milton Erickson believe that responses given are normally through the unconscious mind and they used the case of indirect suggestions as an example. Many of the nonverbal suggestions such as metaphors will mask the true intentions of the hypnotist from the conscious mind of the victim. A form of hypnosis that is completely reliant upon the unconscious theory is subliminal suggestion. Where the unconscious mind is left out in the hypnosis process then this form of hypnosis would be impossible. The distinction between the two schools of thoughts is quite easy to decipher. The first school of thought believe that suggestions are directed at the conscious mind will use verbal suggestions while the second school of thought who believe that suggestions are directed at the unconscious mind will use metaphors and stories that mask their true intentions. In general, the participant will still need to draw their attentions to an object or idea. This enables the hypnotist to lead the participant in the direction that the hypnotist will need to go into the hypnotic state. Once this stage of suggestion is completed and is successful, the participant will move onto the next stage.

Susceptibility

It has been shown that people are more likely to fall prey of the hypnotist tactics than others will. Therefore, it will be noted that some people are able to fall into hypnosis easily and the hypnotist does not have to put so much effort while for some, getting into the hypnotic stage may take longer and require the hypnotist to put quite the effort. While for some even after the continued efforts of the hypnotist they will not get into the hypnotic state. Research has shown where a person has been able to reach the hypnotic state at some point in their lives then it is likely that they will be susceptible to the hypnotist's suggestions and those who have not been hypnotized or it has always been difficult for them to reach that state then it will be likely that they may never be able to reach that hypnotic state.

Different models have been established to determine susceptibility of partakers to hypnosis. Research done by Deirdre Barrett showed that there are two types of subjects that considered being more susceptible to hypnosis and its effects. The two subjects consist of the group of dissociates and fantasizers. Fantasizers are able to easily block out the stimuli from reality without the specific use of hypnosis. They day dream a lot and also spent their childhood believing in the existence of imaginary friends. Dissociates are persons who have scarred childhoods. They have experienced trauma or child abuse and found ways to put away the past and become numb. If a person belongs to this groups finds him or herself day dreaming then it will be associated in terms of being blank and in creation of fantasies. These two groups will have the highest rates of being hypnotized.

Types Of Hypnosis

A hypnotist can use different types of hypnosis a participant. Each of them will use different ways and will help with certain issues. Some types of hypnosis will assist in the area of weight loss while others will be used to help a participant relax. The types of hypnosis are discussed below.

Traditional hypnosis

This type of hypnosis is very popular and used by hypnotists. It works by the hypnotist making suggestions to the participant's unconscious mind. The participant that is likely to be hypnotized by this is one who does what he is told and does not ask many or frequent questions. If one was to self-hypnotise themselves, they will do this by using traditional hypnosis. Like we have said this type of hypnosis is very popular and this could be attributed to it does not require much skill and it is not technical. The hypnotist will just have the right words and just tell the participant what to do. This might pose a problem to the hypnotist where the participant is a critical thinker and is able to analyse a given situation.

Neuro-Linguistic Programming (NLP)

This type of hypnosis gives the hypnotist wide criteria for the methods they can use in the process of hypnosis. The hypnotist is able to save time during the process as the hypnotist will just use the same thought patterns as the one that is creating the problem in the participant. If it is stress for example, the same thought pattern causing this stress will be used to counter the stress. The different types of NLP are discussed below.

NLP Anchoring

To understand how anchoring works, think of a particular scent. The first time you had that scent you were going through some feeling which the unconscious mind attached these feelings to that scent. Through this, the scent will become the anchor for those particular feelings. Every time you heard the scent, those feelings come rushing back triggered by the unconscious mind. This type of NLP has been useful to hypnotists in the process of hypnosis. If for example you won a prize or some money, the hypnotist will try and recreate those feelings you had when you won the prize. While recreating these feelings, the hypnotist will ensure the participant does an action during this process. Each time the subject does the said action, they will be reminded of those feelings.

This type of NLP can be used to motivation a person to accomplish their goals for example if they are trying to be healthier or trying to lose weight. The hypnotist will create a positive anchor that is in line with the mental image of the participant. The mental picture will be that of a sexy slim body. This image will be used as the motivator to start losing weight.

NLP Flash

This technique should only be done by a certified professional because it is considered to be very powerful and used to alter thoughts and emotions around the unconscious mind of the participant. It is considered helpful to persons who experience chronic stress or are addicted to a substance. Here is what the hypnotist will do; he or she where a person is addicted to a substance instead of it causing some feelings of happiness the act will now cause feelings of pain.

Where the person had chronic stress, the cat will bring a sense of relaxation. Those addicted to substances such as cigarettes and alcohol will now feel pain when they take these substances which then can effectively assist them in getting over their addiction. While those undergoing chronic stress will find this technique also very useful as it helps them relax because stress can be very harsh to one's body. They will be able to know what causes their stress and redirect them to cause feelings of relaxation instead. NLP flash has been effective in getting rid of conditioned responses found in the mind of the subject. A practical example will be a person who enjoys drinking alcohol in events. Whenever this person is at an event even where no alcoholic drinks are being served, he will associate every event to alcohol. When this person goes through NLP Flash, they will be to separate these two events from each other. This means the person will be able to enjoy an event without thinking about alcohol and will be effective when trying to quit consuming alcohol.

NLP Reframe

This is the third type of NLP that can be used in hypnosis. It aims and works well in helping the participant change the way they behave. The hypnotist, for this work, should be able to comprehend that there is in fact a positive outcome when the behaviour is changed. The focus on the outcome is critical as this is the reason for using this form of NLP in the first place. Despite this, the behaviour chosen to achieve the outcome is not as important. The process involves the hypnotist trying to engage with the unconscious mind of the participant. The end game is to get the unconscious mind to be responsible for the participant's new chosen behaviour that will help in achieving the secondary gain. This new behaviour will then be more acceptable to the conscious mind of the participant.

Ericksonian Hypnosis

This type of hypnosis uses stories and metaphors. This hypnosis uses stories and metaphors to create ideas and suggestions in the unconscious mind. This hypnosis is very effective and powerful but the only downside it has it is that it requires someone whose experienced and trained for it to work and be effective. What is the reason behind its efficacy? The reason underlying is that it is able to eliminate any resistance to the suggestions of the hypnotist. The metaphors used will be of two types. The first is called isomorphic metaphors. This is a common metaphor that gives steps to the unconscious mind by presenting s somewhat story to the participant that in the end will have a moral ending. The unconscious mind will be able to link the elements coming from the story and the element of the problem situation. An example of a story with a moral ending is the famous story of the 'Boy Who Cried Wolf'. This story was told to children to warn them about what would happen when they continuously lie. The children being told this story will be able to link the telling of lies and the boy who is mentioned in the story. They will be able to see that lies can bring problems and that the child will willingly stop lying to avoid problems. The other metaphor is the intersperse metaphor. Here the command explained in the story is not easily understood by the participant outside their unconscious mind.

Hypnotism is a state of consciousness that involves the focused attention together with the reduced peripheral awareness that is characterized by the participant's increased ability to respond to suggestions that are given.

Major Myths of Hypnotism

Myths are untruths or exaggerations regarding the definition, process, and purpose of something. I will list some myths along with their refutations about hypnotism.

Is Hypnotism Sleeping?

No. The hypnotic trance is a modified state of consciousness called the Alpha state. In this state, other than physiological sleep, there is strong electrical activity in the brain due to the very high level of concentration that the subject is performing. Simplifying hypnosis to the maximum, we can define it as monoideism, that is, absolute focus on the imagination.

Hypnotism Is Conditional

A trusting partnership between the hypnotist and subject is required, so if the subject does not want to be hypnotized, they will not be. In the old days, it was said that the hypnotist became the operator of the mind of the hypnotized subject, but I would say that the hypnotist is another facilitator of the trance. He bridges the conscious mind and the unconscious, thus allowing the subject to access a state of consciousness which allows the subject to experience the full potential of their own mind.

Hypnotism Works

If this is true, 100% of the people who can pay attention are mentally weak. After all, if you "dream awake", have fun reading a good book, "travel" listening to an interesting story, or go to the movies and get emotional about them, you go into a trance.

Have you ever encountered a person who has a lost, seemingly distracted look and when you catch her attention, she takes a little fright? This person is not distracted, in fact, she is hyper-concentrated, that is, in trance.

The truth is that once in a while, our brain "hibernates" for a few minutes to save energy. Have you ever wondered if you needed to be aware of everything you do all the time? Consider someone who drives a car, when he was learning, he found it all complicated – steering, gears, brakes, throttle, clutch and all at the same time!

But now, he operates so unconsciously (or automatically) that he even commits himself to reckless talking on a cell phone while driving. Basically, if a human being is able to concentrate and obey the instructions, he can be hypnotized.

The Hypnotized Subject Will Do Whatever the Hypnotist Says

The human mind is not "mother's house". There are particular moral principles of each person and these principles are obeyed and protected by the subject's unconscious mind. Thus, it is true to say that a hypnotized person will do nothing against their moral principles (religion, family, values, physical integrity), that is, if you would not perform an action while "awake", you will not do so while hypnotized.

The Hypnotized Subject Will Tell All His Secrets to the Hypnotist

Hypnotism is a Physiological Phenomenon

It is a legitimate neuro-physiological phenomenon, where brain functioning has very special characteristics, such as muscle relaxation, anesthesia, dilation of the pupils, and memory enhancement.

During the trance, there are actually changes in the brain and this has already been confirmed in a study by examination of volunteers using an encephalogram. Perhaps in mysticism, there is a little hypnosis, but in hypnosis, there is nothing mystical.

Can a Person Not Return From the Trance?

Back from where? You're not going anywhere. The advantage of being hypnotized is that you can travel the whole world without leaving your body, just with your mind.

Finally, hypnosis is a safe method for both entertainment (street, stage) and clinical applications (hypnotherapy and the like). If you believe in God, see the ability to be hypnotized as a divine gift for your self-improvement, but if you do not believe in a deity, see hypnosis as a very powerful tool that nature has given to the human being to accelerate positive changes in life.

Hypnotism Techniques

There are 3 main techniques of hypnotism used in

clinical treatment. Clinical hypnotism, that is, hypnotism performed in the office by a trained professional, can follow different methodologies or concepts, depending on the line of work of the hypnologist. Today, we will present the three most known lines and their main characteristics:

Conditional Hypnotism:

Created and patented by Luiz Carlos Crozera, conditional hypnosis is a technique used to rid the patient's mind of blockages that directly interfere with his physical and emotional health.

In this technique, deep body relaxation is done so that the patient has a decrease in his brain frequency and, with the purest mind, can be led by the hypnotist to the traumatic records that accompany him. At this point, the professional removes the registered emotional charge, disassociating the trauma from the given situation.

Upon returning from the trance, the patient already has an important behavioral change when faced with what caused him anguish. Thus, the hypnotist uses the post-hypnotic suggestion, a technique that executes the commands inserted during the trance, in order to achieve the best possible results. In conditional hypnosis, the patient does not interact with the hypnotist.

Eriksonian Hypnotism:

In this technique of clinical hypnosis, described by the American psychiatrist Milton Erickson, the patient is suggested to seek within himself new learning that leads to a reformulation of thoughts and truths. Thus, the patient is led to the trance and suggested to relive, in a metaphorical way, the situation that causes him pain and suffering but with a completely different outcome, aiming for the trauma to be forgotten.

The idea is not to change what has been experienced, but to give other responses to the trauma since it is believed that the patient has all the resources necessary to solve his own problems.

Classic Hypnotism:

This method is mostly in disuse because it presents less efficient results than the other methodologies. Classic Hypnosis consists of searching in the memory of the patient for the facts that bring him suffering and making him understand that it is part of the past and should no longer reach the present.

How to Hypnotize Someone Without Them Knowing

Have you ever heard of a method that many claims to be able to achieve through repetitive motions, with the help of pendulums or finger movements, which allows them to stay in a state of trance? Is it possible? Well, some people believe so. Texts produced in Egypt in 1550 BC show evidence that older people already used these practices.

Well, the name of this method is hypnosis and, in fact, this is a psychological state, which brings together several phenomena that occur in our mind, and which can produce different impacts. It can be conducted by a voice and has been used as an instrument in the treatment of different diagnoses.

While there are those who believe in past lives and those who do not, it is true that hypnosis can cause the patient to return to a certain age. For example, hypnosis may return someone up to an "x" age, when he may have contracted some kind of trauma.

Let's look at a situation to illustrate: A patient is in a hypnotized state. The doctor puts his hands on the patient's arm and warns that he is applying an ointment, when in fact, he is not applying anything, he just touches the patient's hands. Despite this, the patient has the feeling that the doctor is actually applying an ointment, even being able to smell the ointment as it passes through a positive olfactory hallucination. The patient, who is hypnotized, really believes the doctor's words.

Another example is the case of a patient who smells a scent. When they smell the gunpowder, if this smell happens to be strongly associated with when they were 10 years of age, then the patient can regress until the age of 10 to try to solve some kind of childhood problem. Not everyone is able to perform this practice because a badly done hypnosis session can cause great harm. This is because hypnosis is not restricted only to the return to time but also the treatment of certain psychological problems, which can be aggravated if not treated by a specialized professional. For this reason, only those who have technical knowledge of the use of hypnosis should practice it.

How to Hypnotize a Person

However, if you would like to learn this technique in order to know the principles of hypnosis and then go deeper into the subject, follow this step-by-step guide:

The first thing to do is to make the person quite relaxed. Sitting comfortably and getting ready for the session in peace is a good start. It is not good to lie down because it can lead to sleep and prevent hypnosis from reaching the person's mind.

The second step is to start speaking very slowly so that the person pays attention to your voice and begins to relax at the same time. Then you can use a pendulum (swing the pendulum at the height of the person's eyes) or your own finger, making repetitive movements also at eye level. You could also use the moving image of a spiral. Continue the movement until you see the person become half asleep.

Ideally, the person should not close his or her eyes. One way that helps create concentration is to blink and focus the mind on what is being said. Talk about certain things, slowly, that cause you to relax and ask the person to imagine a feeling of warmth and comfort all over their body.

You need to always be in touch with the person who will be hypnotized. Ask him to take a deep breath and breathe out slowly through his nose. Ensure that the participant always stays relaxed during the hypnosis.

Ask him to imagine himself levitating and also to pay attention to all parts of his body, trying to perceive any discomfort or pain starting with his head and working downwards. Tell him to let the pain go away. Ask him to repeat this kind of thinking for each part of his body.

As soon as you realize that the patient has reached a state of relaxation, have him imagine a spiral staircase. He should fully visualize this thought and go down the stairs. With every step he takes on that ladder, he must feel he is moving ever deeper into his thoughts. A few steps later, as many as you think necessary, let the patient know that there is a door at the end of the staircase and that it is time for him to cross that door.

The person must open the door and enter the next environment. Direct the person to imagine that this environment is a room, which can be decorated in any way that he would like to imagine. Then direct the thoughts of the person saying that he should look in this room for a place to sit.

Say you will count from 1 to 10 and that, in the end, the participant will be in a deep state of hypnosis. This is the time to ask the questions that will bring the patient to the result that you want to extract from that experience. This is also the time to cause sensations by the suggestion of taste and smell, among others. For example, you can ask him to find some chicken in this room and eat it. The hypnotized person will actually believe and feel the taste of eating the chicken.

After the experience, let him know that he will wake up in a few moments. Ask him to rise from the place where, mentally, he is sitting and walk back down the same path. When he reaches the last step, he will be awake and relaxed. Then count to three and say wake up!

Remember that this experience needs a lot of care and

attention to be put into practice. After all, there are proven cases of poorly done hypnosis practices that have caused mental problems in patients. Therefore, seek the guidance of a professional!

DARK NLP

In the 1970s, psychological researcher John Grinder, coined the term Neuro-Linguistic Programming (NLP) for a mind controlling method to change our conscious thoughts and behaviors as desired. Neuro (mind/information) Linguistic (language/words) Programming (learning/control), simply put it's the art of learning the language of your mind to generate satisfying results. NLP is a lot like a User Manual for the brain, to help you communicate the goals and desires of the unconscious mind to the conscious self. Imagine you are in foreign country and craving chicken wings, so you go to a restaurant to order the same but when the food shows up, it ends up being liver stew because of a failed communication. Humans often fail to recognize and acknowledge their unconscious thoughts and desires because a lot of it gets lost in translation to the conscious self. NLP enthusiasts often exclaim: "the conscious mind is the goal setter, and the unconscious mind is the goal getter". The idea being your unconscious mind wants you to achieve everything that you actually desire but if your conscious mind fails to receive the message, you will never set the goal to achieve those dreams.

NLP was developed using excellent therapists and communicators who had achieved great successes as role models. It's a set of tool and techniques to help your master communication, both with yourself and others. NLP is study of human mind combining thoughts and actions with perception to fulfil their deepest desires. Our mind employs complex neural networks to process information and use language or auditory signals to give it meaning while storing these signals in patterns to generate and store new memories. We can voluntarily use and apply certain tools and techniques to alter our thoughts and actions in achieving our goals. These techniques can be perceptual, behavioral and communicative and used control our own mind as well as that of others.

One of the central ideas of NLP is that our conscious mind has a bias towards a specific sensory system called the "Preferred Representational System (PRS)". Phrases like "I hear you" or "Sounds good" signal an auditory PRS, whereas, phrase like "I see you" may signal a visual PRS. A certified therapist can identify a person's PRS and model their therapeutic treatment around it. This therapeutic framework often involves rapport building, goal setting and information gathering among other activities. NLP is increasingly used by individuals to promote self enhancement, such as self reflection and confidence as well as for social skill development, primarily communication.

NLP therapy or training can be delivered in the form of language and sensory based interventions, using behavior modification techniques customized for individuals to better their social communication and improved confidence and self awareness. NLP therapists or trainers strive to make their client understand that their view and perception of the world is directly associated with how they operate in it, and the first step toward a better future is keen understanding of their conscious self and contact with their unconscious mind. Its paramount to first analysis and subsequently change our thoughts and behaviors that are counterproductive and block our success and healing. NLP has been successfully used in treatment of various mental health conditions like anxiety, phobias, stress and even post traumatic stress disorder. An increasing number of practitioners are commercially applying NLP to promise improved productivity and achievement of work oriented goals that ultimately lead to job progression.

Now, let's look at how NLP works. John Grinder, in association with his student Richard Bandler, conducted a research study on techniques used by Fritz Perls (founder of Gestalt therapy), Virginia Satir (Family therapist) and Milton Erickson (renowned Hypnotherapist). They subsequently analyzed and streamlined these therapy techniques to create a behavioral model for mass application in order to achieve sand reproduce excellence in any field. Bandler, a computer science major, helped develop a "psychological programming language" for human beings. On the basis of how our mind processes information or perceives the external world, it generates an internal "NLP map" of what is going on outside. This internal map is created based on the feedback provided by our sense organs, like the pictures we take in, sounds we hear, the taste in our mount, sensations we feel on our skin and what we can smell. However, with this massive influx of information, our mind selectively deletes and generalizes a ton of information. This selection is unique to every person and is determined by what our mind deems relevant to our situation. As a result, we often miss out on a whole lot of information that can be immediately noticed by someone else right off the bat and we end up with a tiny and skewed version of what is really occurring. For example, take a moment and process this statement: "Person A killed person B", now depending on our circumstances and experiences we will all have our own version of that story. Some might think a "a man killed a woman", or "a lion killed a man" or "a terrorist killed a baby" or "John Doe killed Kennedy" and so on and so forth. Now, there's a method to this madness, whatever story you came up with, realize there is way you got to that story which was driven by our own life experience. Our mind creates an internal map of the situation at hand and then we compare that map with other internal maps from our past that we have stored in our mind. Every person has their own internal "library" based on what is important or relevant to them in accordance with their personality.

Did you ever feel that once your conscious mind makes you aware of what you want to do or gain, suddenly the universe seems to be propping up signs that could help you find your way to get what you want? For example, one day you wake up thinking I need to take my family on a vacation. You go on with your day the same way as you have been for days or weeks, but you suddenly notice a poster on an exciting trip to Florida on your way to work, that you later learnt from your coworker has been up for over a month now. You suddenly see that close to that same Starbucks you visit every day, there is a big travel agency that you had never paid attention to. When browsing the Internet, you will suddenly see travel ads all over your Facebook or ads from Airbnb popping up on your YouTube videos. Now all these may come across as coincidences, but the matter of the fact is those things or signs had been there all along but your mind deleted that information or perception because they were not relevant to you. So as your conscious mind starts connecting the dots between your wishes and the reality of the world, you start picking up on new information that may have already been in plain sight, but you are only tuned into now.

What Is Dark Nlp?

Your personality profile also plays a major role in what

information your mind chooses to exclude and what is processed. People who are more focused on security, they are constantly assessing their situation to determine whether its safe for you or not. On the other hand, people who are more freedom oriented, they tend to think of their situation in terms of options and limitation with no focus on safety at all. Your personality determines what and how you update your mental library and ultimately the meaning you add to these internal maps. For example, a kid looking at a roller coaster is thinking only about the fun of traveling through open space in a cool looking ride and given the opportunity will easily and fearlessly jump on the ride, because his personality is not security oriented. But an adult who is able to focus not only on the fun and excitement of the ride but also it's safety and potential hazards, will think twice before making that same decision.

Here are some prominently used NLP techniques:

Anchoring

A Russian scientist, Ivan Pavlov, conducted an experiment on dogs by repeatedly ringing a bell while the dogs were eating and concluded that he could get the dogs to salivate by the ringing the bell anytime, even when there was no food present. This neurobiological connection observed in the dogs, between the bell and salivation is called a conditioned response or "anchor". Thus, the process of creating a perceivable sensory trigger to the state of how you feel is called Anchoring.

Try this yourself! Think of a gesture or sensation on your body (pulling your earlobe, cracking your knuckles, or touching your forehead) and associate it with any desired positive emotional response (happiness, confidence, calmness etc.) by recalling and reliving the memory when you actually experienced those emotions. The next time you are feeling stressed or low, you can trigger this anchor voluntarily and you will notice your feeling will immediately change. To strengthen triggered response, you can think of another memory when your felt the desired emotion and relive it. Every time you add a new memory to the mix, your anchor will become more potent and trigger a stronger response.

Content Reframing

This NLP technique is best suited to combat negative thoughts and feelings. With the use of this visualization techniques you can alter your mind to think differently about situations where you feel threatened or disempowered. Simply view the negative situation and reframe it's meaning into something positive. For example, let's say you just broke up with your long term girlfriend or boyfriend. You will most likely be hurt and in pain. But you can choose to reframe the end of your relationship with empowering thoughts of being single and new potential relationships. You can choose to focus on the lessons you learnt from your past relationship and how you can implement them to have an even better relationship in future. Thus, by simply reframing the break up, you can feel better and empower yourself.

This technique has massive appeal in treatment of post

traumatic stress disorder and for people who have experienced child abuse or are suffering from chronic or life threatening diseases.

Rapport Building

Rapport is the art of generating empathy in others by pacing and mirroring their verbal and non-verbal behaviors. People like other people who they think are similar to themselves. When you can subtly mirror the other person, their brain will fire off "mirror neurons" or "pleasure sensors" in their brain, which make them feel a sense of liking for you. You can simply stand or sit the way the other person or tilt your head in the same direction as theirs or the best of all, just smile when they smile. All these cues will help you build rapport with the other person. The social significance of rapport building cannot be underscored. Strong personal and professional connections lead to a happier and longer life.

Dissociation

The NLP technique of dissociation guides you in severing the link between negative emotions and the associated trigger. For instance, certain words or phrases may instantly bring back bad memories and make you feel stressed or depressed. If you can successfully identify those triggers and make an effort to detach those negative feelings from it, you are one step closer to healing and empowering yourself. A slew of mental health conditions like anxiety, depression and even phobias can be effectively treated with this technique. It can also be used to positively deal with difficult situations at home and work.

Future Pacing

The NLP technique of leading the subject to a future state and rehearsing the potential future outcomes so as to achieve the desired outcome automatically, is called Future Pacing. It's a type of visualization technique or mental imagery, used to anchor a change or resources to future situations by imagining and virtually experiencing those situations. A skilled manipulator can lead their victim on a mental journey into the future and influence the responses occurring when the future unfolds. An expert NLP user with prominent Dark Psychological traits may cognitively transport their victim into the future and suggest outcomes while monitoring the victim's response to eventually get their own desired outcome into the psyche of the victim.

Influence and Persuasion

This is definitely the most ambivalent NLP technique and houses a gray area between Dark Psychology and Psychotherapy. NLP is primarily focused on eliminating negative emotions, curb bad habits and resolve conflicts, another aspect of NLP deals with ethically influencing and persuade others. Now pay attention to the word ETHICAL here.

One of the prominent psychology therapist to participate in Grinder's original research on NLP was, Milton Erickson, leading hypnotherapist and founder of the "American Society for Clinical Hypnosis". Erickson was so adept at hypnosis that he could literally hypnotize anyone anywhere and communicate with people's subconscious mind without needing hypnosis. He helped construct the "Milton Model" of NLP, designed to induce trance like state in people, using abstract language patterns. According to the Milton Model, using artfully vague and deliberately ambiguous sentences will trigger the person to search for meaning of what they hear from their own life experiences and fill in the details subconsciously. This powerful tool can be used to not only ethically influence and persuade people but also help people deal with some deep seated negative emotions, overcome fears and increase their self awareness.

COVERT EMOTIONAL MANIPULATION

Today, the greatest battles are not fought on battlefields, but in our minds and hearts!

And one of the biggest and strongest reasons for an inner battle is psychological manipulation. The biggest problem with psychological manipulation is not only the fact that we are often not prepared to deal with it but also the way we respond to it. And then, our greatest enemy, beyond the manipulator/oppressor, will become ourselves!

One of the main characteristics of psychological manipulation is that the manipulator (who can be a father, a mother, a brother or sister, a romantic partner, or a friend) exercises great control and power over us. And in that instant, our life becomes a real hell and we live in tremendous anguish.

However, it is crucial to know that we are not, and should not be, impotent in this situation and that there are various ways of combating these techniques of psychological manipulation.

The first step is to achieve consciousness, that is, to become aware of these techniques. Take a closer look and learn more objectively how your handlers "work" so you can protect yourself in the future. There are several Manipulation Techniques. See some of them below:

Psychological Manipulation Technique 1: Emotional Blackmail

Emotional blackmail is one of the oldest and most used manipulation techniques employed by human beings. But how does this work exactly?

Many people succumb to this trick because they feel they have no choice. At this point, phrases such as "If you really cared about me, you would do this for me" are very common and make the manipulated person feel "forced" to make decisions that they do not really want. The target will make them anyway just to please the person who manipulates.

To avoid this manipulation technique you will have to develop a strong sense of your own self, and this involves knowing who you are, what your responsibilities are towards others, and who your true friends are. Usually, manipulative and blackmailing people tend to stay away from people with strong and solid personalities. Always remember: you always have a choice and it is you who decides what you do with your life and how you want to react to the world.

Psychological Manipulation Technique 2: Focus on Negative Aspects

Some people like to put a "brake" on another's ideas and brilliant projects by emphasizing everything that could go wrong with them. These people often push him to doubt his projects and all the good things they would bring if they were put into practice. And at these times, the manipulators offer an endless list of questions that will only serve to create and raise doubts in their target's mind and heart.

For example, if you are telling someone you are thinking of traveling somewhere for a month to relax or go on vacation, and if for some reason that person does not feel comfortable with the idea, they will probably react to your news by talking about the immense travel hazards and the endless number of negative things that can be expected at the airport, etc., etc.

At such times, if there is no apparent reason for such a reaction from the other person. If you are comfortable with your decision, bearing in mind that it will not harm you or others, choose not to listen to them and follow through with what you have decided.

Do not be overly swayed by this negative thinking pattern because if we think about something a lot, we attract it. That is, if you put it in your head that something bad will happen and focus on it excessively, it is very likely to happen because the thought has life and is a great magnet.

Psychological Manipulation Technique 3: Teenage Rebellion

Unfortunately, sometimes the manipulative person adopts a childlike attitude as a response to his decision, or something you have said to him.

For example, you want to leave your home and live independently. At first, it may even seem like everyone is happy and comfortable with your decision. But with the passage of time, as soon as you start looking for the perfect apartment, things start happening one after another. Some kind of personal crisis occurs in the family, your mother or father suddenly (re) starts smoking, etc. These are adult people, but they adopt the behavior of a teenager and rebel against the idea.

The easiest way to deal with this is to make them see that their efforts in trying to make you give up are worthless and that you will go ahead with your decision.

At first, it can be very difficult and hard for you, especially if you have been exposed to this type of psychological manipulation for a long time. But as time goes by, it will become much easier and you will see that even the people who manipulate you will come to respect you much more.

Psychological manipulation can be done throughout life, but always remember that you have the power to break this vicious cycle and above all, remember that only one person can change your life: You!

Love and life together can be sources of well-being, pleasure, and support or a dead end in which you feel suffocated and as if you are in the dark. The worst is that in many cases, these can be combined in a single day. Both feelings and problems begin when the relationship shifts rapidly and you find yourself immersed in a constant storm of feelings. This mainly happens to those who do not know how to escape such situations.

Many people are immersed in insane and toxic relationships in which they suffer psychological abuse of various kinds. They receive continuous damage to their integrity and their honor and levels of disrespect that when seen or heard from outside seem crazy, but to the person who is now accustomed to suffering, does not even produce a minimal reaction in their daily lives.

Love is not an excuse to hide the emotional pain that another person can cause us, and it is our responsibility to ourselves to learn how to defend our rights and enforce them. Beyond your own insecurity, the parental patterns that you picked up in your childhood, and all the mechanisms of self-deception that you are capable of activating so as not to see reality, at the bottom of your being, you know how to differentiate what is right and what hurts you. That said, sometimes we need someone to tell us in a neutral and unbiased way that we have the right not to put up with what we know we do not deserve. Next, I present a list of the main techniques of manipulation in unhealthy couples.

Manipulation to maintain social control: This technique usually begins in a very subtle way. The couple criticizes friends, family, work colleagues and anyone in your social circle until they can completely annul the other's social network in such a way that the only source of effort and social support is the couple. This is manifested through jealousy: "If you really love me, you would prefer me over your friends" etc.

Emotional blackmail: This mechanism is famous for being used between pairs of individuals. It is also widely used by almost everyone and you likely know it very well. It is about using phrases to handle guilt and repentance as a tactic to get something or as an impediment so that the other does not do something or does not abandon the manipulator. The manipulative person usually uses phrases like: "If you do that, it means you don't love me", "I do not want you to suffer, I would never do that to you", "I want the best for you, even if you let me destroy my life", "If you let me die", etc.

Mental manipulation techniques: These are the most

creative and there are many types. The manipulator frequently attempts to put the other person into some type of debt to them or does things that have a lot of intensity so that the victim feels a commitment to that person. These phrases help explain the main idea and are things the manipulator will often say: "Only someone who loves you very much will do this for you", "No one will love you like me", etc. It is also a manipulation technique to mentally "vaccinate" the other person to things people in their environment might say by mentioning things like: "Your family hates me, but they do not know what love is", "They will speak ill of me, they will tell you that this relationship does not work", or "It's convenient, but I love you like nobody else", etc. These phrases echo in the head of the manipulated person and confuse and influence their behavior.

Intermittent reinforcement guidelines: This manipulation technique is designed to get the couple to overestimate the pleasant moments that the other-the one who manipulates-offers. For this, what he does-whether consciously or unconsciously-is to have arguments and fights over small things so that afterward, there is reconciliation and more intensity is created in the relationship. This technique is very addictive because of the pleasant stimuli, reconciliation, that appears after the unpleasant stimuli. This is as addictive to our brain as one of those slot machines because the couple is totally unpredictable and the person ends up living in a world of fights waiting for each reconciliation. The person usually thinks "I suffer, but I know that everything is going to be fixed".

In the psychology of learning, we call it "intermittent reinforcement patterns", it is a simple mechanism: Fight-suffering-tears / reconciliation-passionate love-sex- and start again for a new fight. Periods of peace and "Honeymoons" start becoming less and less frequent and become shorter in duration. This mechanism is so powerful that if the person leaves the relationship, he will miss it and it will create self-esteem problems. It is also difficult for the abandoned person to forget the other. The addiction is established when the subject continues to play despite losing because he has the memory in his head that he once won, so he will continue to insist on continuing even though the prizes are minimal compared to the effort to "play".

Techniques designed to reduce self-esteem: This type of technique usually appears once the social network of the other person has been damaged and now the couple is the main or only support system the person has. It is usually based on insulting, criticizing, ridiculing, weaving a network of lies before third parties about that person, giving no rewards to things and initiatives that the other has by discounting their importance, diminishing their merits or pleasing actions, and focusing conversations on everything that person does wrong or lacks. The most common are phrases like "I would be better off without you" and "Without me you are nobody".

Another very frequent way to diminish self-esteem is to make the other person feel guilty by using criticism and shame with phrases like "I did not expect that from you", etc. The manipulator may also adopt an active role in the victim's life, making decisions for them or taking care of many activities that require effort. This causes the victim's coping mechanisms for facing life to be less and less effective because they get used to the comfort of being with someone who does things for them and solves problems. This technique can cause the person to feel that they must depend on the other person in some important aspect or even for less important things such as making purchases, making food, keeping household accounts, etc

Stereotyped Roles: This technique is based on playing specific characters within the couple. The most frequent within the couple is usually: The role of the savior, victim, or persecutor. The person with the role of the victim usually manipulates with expressions of jealousy, crying, and stimulation of emotions of grief in the other person. The role of the savior is the person who seeks in the couple someone to protect, seeking recognition for it. The persecutor is usually vigilant, critical, and points out all the mistakes of the other person.

Self-destructive acts: This manipulation mechanism consists of anything that a subject does that cause physical or psychological damage to themselves. The aim is to produce in another person a feeling of guilt, grief, and emotional blackmail. It can also be breaking a material object in the victim's presence, self-coupling, or doing it in front of another person who knows the victim so that it reaches their ears. These self-destructive behaviors create strong feelings of guilt and make it difficult for the person to disassociate from the manipulative partner. The manipulator may even say things like: "If you leave, I will kill myself."

Compulsive acts aimed at revenge and the creation of fear: This consists of doing things that the person knows will hurt the other to continue emotional intensity. This mechanism is also aimed at keeping the relationship together because it generates strong feelings of fear of possible reprisals or negative consequences of deciding to leave the couple.

These are some of the main techniques used in unhealthy relationships to maintain control in the other person. In spite of living in a continuous battle and suffering, such relationships usually last for years before they are perceived as harmful enough to warrant leaving, even though the two parties that make up the couple usually suffer very intensely.

If you have identified with the behaviors discussed above, surely you have suffered psychological abuse and may even use that same pattern on your partner. People are like mirrors, we reflect everything that surrounds us and it is common that in this type of unhealthy relationship both parties are exercising some kind of manipulation.

It is not about looking for the guilty party or attempting to demonize the other. In a relationship, all the participants contribute to the result and end up feeling the consequences in one way or another. In an unhealthy relationship, nobody wins or is better than the other and in most cases, people simply do the only thing they know how to do and project their own problems on the other person. Therefore, understanding the dynamics of the couple is one of the most important means we have for personal development. Finally, we each have an important lesson to learn about ourselves; if we are able to discover it before the link is completely broken and if both are open to change, it would be possible to perform couples therapy. Although in most cases, emotional breakdowns are so painful and the destruction in different areas of the lives of the people involved in the relationship is so extensive that ending the relationship is more likely. Reconciliation is often seen as difficult as there is a need to invest in a personal change to continue with that partner.

Between the banks of pain and pleasure flows the river of life. Only when the mind refuses to flow with life and stagnates on the banks does it become a problem. Flow means acceptance, letting come what comes, letting go what is meant to go.

Persuasion is never without moral implications but in dark persuasion moral implications are just not the determining factor. There are many other factors which are more important than being morally correct. The smartest thing about a dark persuader is that in their circle they would be the most selfish person but would show and seem that they are least selfish. They would get exactly what they get, without the other person knowing or even realizing.

The other thing that a dark persuader does is knowing about the weakness of others. This helps them in extracting words, presents, and gifts which they can take or give according to their advantage and situation. For example, if an employer knows that he has illegal immigrants working in his company, he can always lower his wages as per his choice as they know that they cannot work anywhere else in the country.

Dark persuasion can vary from small to very large

scale, such as a kid asking his elder brother for all the ice cream he has to a leader trying to ask for help in war to defeat another country. So, to determine dark persuasion it is always vital to understand the different personalities and their circumstances.

Covert manipulation is even worse than manipulation, in this, the manipulator tries to use the emotional vulnerability to their benefit. They would strive to their best so that they can know about your goals, strengths, weaknesses, fear, family, etc. So that they can use all of these factors to make you feel low and weak. It is said to be underhanded methods of control. It operates under your level of conscious awareness. The bad part of it is that the victim is not even aware that they are being manipulated, that is the reason it becomes prime for you to know about the manipulation games that these people use, which we will discuss later in coming chapters.

Covert manipulation is very dangerous as it is so subtle and underhanded that it takes a long time before you can make out that you were being manipulated. According to research, it was also found that there are few manipulators with such sharp skills that they are called puppet masters, you would without even knowing become their puppets, so it is important for you to know their signs so that you can take the actions accordingly. They would make you feel that you are doing according to your own wish but the truth is that you do that only what they ask you to do.

Sometimes you might feel that something is wrong but you would not be able to analyze that someone is trying to manipulate you. In covert manipulation first thing which is prime is that you should ask yourself if you are being manipulated? As covert manipulation is adverse and has a negative effect on us, so it would be easier for you to understand that you are being manipulated.

It is significant for you to understand a few characteristics of a covert manipulator, so it becomes really easy for you to spot them if they are around you-

Lying- They would lie straight in your eyes and you would not even get to know that they are lying. They would tell you twisted truth or half-truth which you might or might not get to know later. If you ever have any doubts on the other person about the truth, you should always double-check the information so that it does not hamper your relationship or work.

Backhanded compliments- This is something they are best at. Covert manipulators are great in giving backhanded compliments. They would give compliments as you did it in a great way although you are so weak and low in confidence, still, you handled it well. You cooked so well, although you do not cook for me often. These compliments make you feel even more embarrassed and awkward, where you do not even know how to react. In such cases, the best thing is to ignore or giving them the taste of their own medicine by replying in the same way.

Mirroring- The coincidences would be extravagant. They would agree to all your points, likes, dislikes, taste, color, etc just to impress you or to be with you. When they want to take benefit from you they would agree to all your things and choices. Once they get what they wanted everything would change. You would feel that the person has fully switched. So, you should always beware of the person who agrees to whatever you say without keeping their point of you, it straight away means that they are trying to be manipulative.

Rationalization- This is something many people would do to cover their lies or fault. They would cook new stories to cover their flaws such as the reason why you did not tell that you had a girlfriend before me, the reason they would give you would be like I did not want to lose you by telling this or I did not know how you would react after listening to this, etc. Thu they would have answers for all the lies, so make sure that you know and follow your gut feel to analyze if he is saying right or just faking it.

Hurried Intimacy- This is a very alarming sign of a covert manipulator. They would very quickly tell you about their goals, achievements, passion and past and what ask you the same things. Once you open up with them, they would use this information to control and manipulate you. Therefore, you should always be wise enough to understand when to share the information and how much information to share. They would be very quick in proposing for marriage and talking about the future but you need to be careful before telling your weaknesses.

Playing the victim- This is another thing they do to

gain your sympathy. Just to gain your love and attention they would lie to you to any extent. They might say that their childhood was very bad as the parents were not good, etc. Just to get more love and care from you. They might make any stories for your love and care, so always know the past first before you get so much involved.

Silent Treatment- Leaving room or house for a couple of hours, would not engage in any activity, etc. They also hide behaviors or start avoiding you so that you realize it is your mistake or you start the conversation. They keep the concerns unspoken within them which is a dangerous sign too.

Belittling- They do react weird such as rolling the eyes, scoffing, mocking, teasing, etc. They do not even respect others point of view or abilities, and they always want another person to feel low and always try to demean them. You should always maintain a distance with such covert people who are jealous of your success and feel bad seeing you rise.

Word Play- A covert manipulator very well knows what you want to hear and would please your ears by saying that. They know how to put a convincing statement, paint the picture well and also to induce an emotional reaction in front of you. Not only this, they are great it talking double meaning things, they would mean something else but say it in a different context. For example, please marry me I will change your life. This can be in any aspect positive or negative. So be precise and clear while talking to a covert manipulator.

Finance controller- Covet manipulator not only restrict by playing with your emotions they are also good in controlling and gaming with your finances too. For example, accessing your account but denying access to their account, taking things on loan in joint names without even asking you, running up debts, borrowing and not paying, etc. These are very tricky things which you should be careful about and take a step in time before they make your account nil.

These were the few characteristics of a covert manipulator which you should be diligent about so that nobody can take advantage of you or humiliate you.

BRAINWASHING

In this guidebook, brainwashing is better discussed in psychological terms and how it is associated via social influences. Talking about social influences, it is the collective approaches used for influencing or changing other people's beliefs, attitudes and behavior toward something. Be that as it may, brainwashing could actually be characterized as a social issue in a severe form since it functions at changing the perspective of a subject without the subject agreeing to it.

To carry out a successful brainwashing, the subject has to be totally isolated and dependent since it has an invasive effect on the subject. This explains why most cases of brainwashing happen in prison camps or totalistic cults. The agent or brainwasher needs to gain complete control of the subject. He or she must be in absolute command of their subject's sleeping patterns and eating habits whilst satisfying the other vital needs of the subject, and none of these happen without the knowledge of the brainwasher. While the procedure takes place, the agent seeks for ways to break down the subject's entire identity, so it doesn't work right anymore. From the moment that identity is broken, the brainwasher strives to exchange it with the desired attitudes, beliefs and behaviors.

The idea of brainwashing is not generally agreed upon by everybody. If it works or not isn't certain yet, as many people have different opinions about it. Some psychologists believe that if the right conditions are in place, brainwashing a subject is possible. However, the entire task is never as severe as portrayed in the media. Several definitions of brainwashing exist which makes it really tough to know the consequences of brainwashing on a victim. Most definitions require the presence of some form of threat to the physical body of the victim for it to be called brainwashing. In line with this definition, most practices carried out by extremist cults would not be regarded as real brainwashing since physical abuse was absent.

The remaining definitions of brainwashing make use of control and coercion with no physical force, while aiming at getting the subject to change his/her beliefs. Whichever definition it is, pundits agree that even with all the conditions in place, the results of brainwashing lasts for just a brief moment. Experts also agree that the former identity of the victim is never erased totally with the experience; instead, it is sent into hiding and re-surfaces when the new identity is no longer forced upon the victim again.

Robert Jay Lifton presented fascinating opinions on brainwashing in the 1950s after observing prisoners of the Korean and Chinese War camps. During his studies, he concluded that his subjects (prisoners) went through several stages in brainwashing. These stages start with an attack on the victim's self-concept and conclude with a supposed change in beliefs of the prisoner. Lifton defined 10 steps for the brainwashing process in the prisoners he studied. These steps are:

Attack the subject's identity;

Force guilt on the subject;

Force self-betrayal on the subject;

Reach a breaking point;

Offer the subject leniency if they change;

Compulsory confession;

Point all the guilt in the intended direction;

Liberate the subject from supposed guilt;

Move into harmony;

A last confession before a rebirth.

These steps must be carried out in a completely isolated area. What this means is that all the regular social references the victim is used to coming in contact with are not available. Furthermore, mind clouding schemes like starvation and sleep deprivation will be utilized in order to speed up the procedure. Even though this may not be what's obtainable in all cases of brainwashing, there' is often the presence of some kind of bodily harm. This makes it difficult for the subject to think critically and independently like they usually do.

Different Techniques Of Brainwashing

As we now understand, brainwashing doesn't occur overnight but is usually a series of actions taken simultaneously over a period of time, which eventually results into a changed personality. Perception and behavior change, sometimes to such an extent that the victim becomes unrecognizable to their friends or peers.

The techniques used and the speed with which the personality changes depends on many things, but most of all on whether the target is being subjected to brainwashing against their will (in which case they'll naturally resist as much as they can) or whether they don't know they're being brainwashed (e.g. in cults) and believe all the ideas being impressed upon them are their own and that they themselves are making the decisions. This could be deemed successful brainwashing, as the victim is unaware of what's occurring.

Most common overt and covert brainwashing techniques:

- **Repetition and nagging**

  It's hard not to start believing something or at least begin doubting one's self if someone is constantly repeating the same thing over and over every day, for months or even years.

- **solation**

  It is easier to control someone if they have no access to sources of information which conflict with the brainwashing material. If the target talks to someone about the ideas being imposed upon them and other people understand what's happening, they may scupper the chances for a successful brainwash. This tactic is often witnessed in abusive relationships, where one partner doesn't want the other to communicate with friends or family incase their motives are uncovered.

- **Blind obedience**

This prevents the victim from thinking for themselves.

- **Responsibility**

One central brainwashing technique is to make someone feel responsible for their faults and the things that go wrong in their life. If they make mistakes, do something poorly, or if things don't go according to plan, making them feel responsible leaves them feeling negative emotions such as guilt and shame, which lowers their defenses and opens them up for manipulation.

- **Guilt and fear**

These are used extensively as part of an overall emotional manipulation plan. When a huge guilt complex is imposed, we start believing we're deserving of any resulting punishment.

Self-brainwashing techniques:

Identify a negative thought pattern

Identify a negative thought or belief that's been holding you back. How long have you felt this way? Can you connect the programming to any early life experiences? Are you aware of how this belief has affected your life? What do you think your life would have been like if it weren't for this negative thought pattern? Do you believe you are what others tell you? What skills or abilities do you wish you had?

Acknowledging the damage

Be aware of any negative emotional, mental or physical harm this thought pattern has done to you, then make the decision to do something about it. Negative programming can be reversed, but it takes time, so be prepared to work on this issue for a long time if need be.

The Power of Suggestion

Much of our negative thinking comes from suggestions we take in from others. Think of how many times someone has spoken to you negatively, said you were fat, stupid or unintelligent? Eventually, when these suggestions are heard repeatedly they tend to became our reality.

We can reverse such damage by purposefully taking our suggestions onto a more positive path by consciously choosing positive beliefs. Whatever flaws you believe you have, they can often be reversed. One such way is to constantly tell yourself what you'd like to become, by verbally affirming (or thinking) how successful, healthy or confident you are. Eventually, with commitment, these suggestions can come true as our actions and behaviors gradually begin to follow the constant positive reinforcement we're feeding ourselves.

Repetition

Repetition is successfully used in self-brainwashing. Consistently reinforce positive thoughts about yourself or your self-image by repeating confidence-boosting words and affirmations throughout the day. If it helps, use sticky notes on your desk, inside your car, on the fridge, and other places where you'll often see them. Or, try chanting short phrases such as, 'I am smart', 'I am successful', 'People like me' or whatever you're trying to change.

DECEPTION

It is about time we moved onto our first form of mind control: deception. You will see a lot of similarities between deception and manipulation as you continue reading. One of the reasons is that both are types of covert mind control systems, so, the aims and processes are somehow similar. Again, manipulative people are known to deploy a lot of deception so as to achieve their goals.

What Is Deception?

Deception is identified as the act of misleading, promoting an idea, concept, or belief that is false or simply hiding the truth. If someone is 25 years old and says they are 30 years old, they are committing the act of deception. As humans, we deceive others a lot of times. Even the people we consider as honest deceive others or themselves several times a day, according to various studies. Deceiving others may not necessarily be a bad thing as it can help to avoid negative situations. In society, some lies can be used to maintain proper functioning as long as no negative consequences arise from the deception. For example, if the police announce that they will conduct swoops on places frequented by idle youth so as to keep them off the streets yet fail to do it; we can refer to this as a necessary form of deception.

In the context of our book, however, we are talking about the dark type of deception which has the potential to cause harm to other people. Therefore, we can add to the definition of deception as the act of concealing the truth and making people believe in falsehood for selfish benefits while exposing them to harm. So, if a child lies about being chased by a dog as the reason for coming late to school, they are not exposing the teacher to any harm. Even if the deceit was discovered, it would only spell more punishment to the student. When we are talking about harmful deception, it is the one where the agent promotes falsehood to gain an advantage over their victim. If such deceit is detected, it risks harming the subject more than the agent.

Let us have an example of harmful deception.

A story is told about three elementary school kids who

were at a park on a night in the 1980s when police were called about a woman who had been found raped and badly beaten. Upon getting to the scene, the police took the woman to a hospital as others went searching inside the vast park for any clues or suspects. At the far end of the park, they saw the three young boys sitting under some trees while sipping booze and laughing. Without conducting any proper inquiries, the police immediately arrested the boys on the assumption that they had committed the offense.

At the police station, the leading investigator wrote a statement claiming the boys were found near the unconscious woman and were laughing about the matter when the police found them. The woman had suffered severe trauma to the head that led to memory loss and inability to speak well. Therefore, she could not confirm or deny whether the three boys were her attackers. The only evidence that existed was semen on the woman's undergarments and the fact that the boys were at the park on the same night of the abuse. Unfortunately for the boys, the judge believed the police and imprisoned each of them to 25 years in jail.

10 years later, a man approached the judge who had convicted the boys and confessed to having attacked the woman. At this time, DNA technology had emerged. Upon comparing the DNA on the semen found on the woman with that of the man, they matched. He confessed to having been on a revenge mission after the woman walked out on their marriage. The young men were set free after spending 10 years in undeserving incarceration.

Upon further investigations, it was found that the police officer who had lied about finding the boys near the woman and laughing at their actions had been under pressure to reduce crime in his area of work. To prove his effectiveness, he had lied about the young boys. This act not only deceived the judge into jailing the innocent men but also proving to his superiors and community that he was an effective officer. The judge apologized as the officer was sent to prison.

From this story, we can see that deception aims at tricking and fooling the other party for personal gains. We can assume that if the officer were not under pressure to prove his worth, he would not have lied about the boys. To him, the crime at the park presented itself as an opportunity to redeem his career without caring about the consequences that his actions would have on the victims.

It is also evident that dark deception may take some time before it is discovered. At times, it may not, at all. However, in the event that it is discovered, it leads to devastating consequences for both the victims and the offender. In this case, the three men had been suffering for a crime they did not commit. Even though they were set free, the 10 years they had lost were not going to be recovered. The judge, too, felt guilty of sending the innocent kids to jail and had to apologize. The perpetrator, too, was affected in that he was punished for deceiving the justice system.

In summary, deception in the context of dark psychology benefits the deceiver more than the subject. The deception can be used to create a relationship between the two, allowing the deceiver entry into the subject's mind. Once a relationship is created, the deceiver starts exploiting their victim and extracting their benefits.

Primary Components Of Deception

Manipulators such as liars are aware that trust is the strongest bond that can exist between two people.

Therefore, they usually create it between them and their victim before they initiate their mind control process. On the other hand, when the victim trusts the deceiver, this act is equivalent to dropping the guard that prevents them from being controlled without their knowledge. If we can go back to our story, we know the judge trusted the investigating police officer. In the judge's mind, police officers are sworn to be truthful. As such, when he was told that the boys were found near the unconscious lady and that they had been laughing about their actions, he was bound to believe it. In short, the officer had betrayed the trust and influenced the judge's mind.

The saddest part about deception is that it utilizes the trust to harm the victim. This makes it very painful for the victim when they realize it. In a way, they perceive themselves as having been fooled and actually assisting the agent in taking advantage of them. Trust, like many emotions, has the ability to convince people to do things which they would not do if it had not existed. For example, in e-commerce, people purchase things on a pre-order basis. This is mainly because they trust the companies that offer products such as Apple. If apple were a new company with no reputation online, people would not pay for items that they have not seen or touched. This trust is what deceivers use to access their victims and control them as they wish.

Evidently, trust is the emotion that enables the agent to control the victim. The victim believes in the deceiver and might even base future plans on the deception. All this time, everything the deceiver will be saying or doing is false. Another thing the deceiver is aware of is that the trust can be ruined in case the subject finds out that they have been lied to. Therefore, they need to be good at turning things around so as to reduce their chances of being found out. More characteristics of deceivers are listed below.

The Process of Deception

The overall concept of deceit is to propagate a false sense of reality, such as a story so that the target believes it and then later doing something totally different. That said, the process of deception can be divided into three parts, as explained below:

The Objective

Before finding their potential targets, deceivers first come up with the end goal (objective) in mind. For instance, a con artist decides what they want to get from someone. It might be money, a valuable item, or personal favors. Their type of objective is critical in the entire deception planning process. Once they have the end goal in mind, they work backward to find out what needs to be done to achieve it.

Identifying Potential Targets

Once the goal is set, they go to identifying the most vulnerable type of people. Just like animals in the wild prefer the most vulnerable prey such as the young, aged, sickly, injured or weakest, a deceiver is also very careful when choosing his or her prey. Back to the example of the con artist, assuming their goal is to steal credit card details from someone, they might prefer going for older people who are not conversant with online purchases. An elderly person is easier to deceive on the internet than a young one.

Studying the Target

Once the deceiver has identified the potential target, they start the process of studying them. The aim here is to figure out the target's vulnerabilities and strengths. These include their capabilities, strongest emotions, capabilities, beliefs, preconceptions, social and family status, and so on. If they are successful in "predicting" the vulnerability of their targets, they know exactly where to hit so as to improve their efficiency. At this stage, they move in to create trust as the technique to reduce suspicion and gain control of the target's mind.

Settling on the Best Technique

The final stage of the deception planning process is to formulate the story or the most appropriate form of deception.

This four-step process might appear like it takes weeks or months to plan, but it can even be made in a few minutes. A good example is when a bully wants to steal another person's property. Although the planning process might take a few minutes, it adheres to the above template.

The Trojan horse Story

Let us use the story of the Greek Trojan horse to understand this process better.

The Greeks had attempted to invade and destroy the Troy (Trojan) City for close to a decade without any success. When it finally dawned on them that invading Troy was not going to be easy, they decided to apply a different strategy. This strategy was going to involve mind control. At this point, we can easily decode the objective of the Greeks as invading Troy and winning the war.

Next, the Greeks decided to lure the Troy army by faking retreat. They knew that by retreating, the Troy army would assume the war was over and drop their guard. This was seen as the best plan as opposed to their previous ambush method, which had failed for a decade. At this point, again, we see the Greeks identifying their target's vulnerability.

The third step was studying the target and creating trust with them. To earn the Trojans' trust, the Greeks decided to "gift" them with a symbol that would represent their withdrawal. The gift was a large wooden horse that could house a number of Greek soldiers inside. When the Trojans saw the horse, they were happy and believed the Greeks had given up victory in their favor. To add to the manipulation, the Greeks sailed their ships away.

As the Greeks sailed away, the Trojan army moved the wooden horse into their city. Unknown to them, the horse contained some skilled Greek soldiers. That night, as the city slept, the soldiers jumped out of the horse and opened the city gates. The ships had also come back, and the entire Greek army ambushed the city and destroyed it. We can say the Greeks had settled on the technique of diversion or, to some extent, dazzling. Eventually, they achieved their goal.

Detecting Deception

Detecting any form of mind control, leave alone deception, can be hard owing to the wit of the toxlc people as well as the carefully planned processes they use. Most of the time, the deception will show up once the goal has been achieved or if the deceiver missteps and blows their cover. Otherwise, if the liar is a good one, they will juggle with the subject's mind until they have achieved their objectives. Therefore, detecting deception can be difficult since there are no accurate or reliable indicators that can detect when deception is happening.

As hard as it might seem to detect deception, there might be a few loopholes that present themselves during the process. According to psychologists, deceiving others can place a large load on the perpetrator since they need to keep their covers perfectly hidden. To some extent, they need to fight with the notion of deceiving themselves while trying to control their subjects. The risk of missing a single step and making the subject suspicious usually overwhelms the deceiver. Therefore, at some point in the deception process, hints might be dropped, albeit subconsciously. Some of the clues are verbal, while the rest are non-verbal such as body language.

Aldert Vrij, a scholar who studies deception, there are no specific tell-tale signs that may suggest that deception is happening. There may be a few clues, though, but they risk being confused with other traits that represent different ideas. Therefore, the surest way to tell if a manipulator is using deception is when they are caught.

The lack of definite methods of detecting deception does not mean we should ignore potential signs that may indicate something fishy is happening. Psychologists have come up with several verbal and non-verbal clues that can occur during the process of deception. Let us have a look at some of them.

Characteristics of Deceivers

They are Manipulative

Deceivers are known to be manipulative people. They can switch between situations and personalities so they can persuade others, through covert force, to fulfill their selfish goals. A normal lie does not require a person to pre-condition the other so they can succeed. Rather, words or actions, usually not pre-planned, are used. However, a pragmatic deceiver displays manipulative traits. In a relationship, for instance, the lover who is always forcing the other to change their ways so they can be satisfied is more likely to be a deceiver. Frequent lies usually build up to chronic manipulation. In short, a person who displays a manipulative character is an obvious deceiver.

They are Good Actors

A person who is good at deceiving others is a definite actor. Acting is the process of putting up a false show, either physically or psychologically. A good actor can arm themselves with false behaviors or stories to convince their subjects. For example, a healthy person can feign illness and ask the public or their friends for money to seek medical attention. If they are not good actors who can change their voices, looks, and mood, they risk not convincing others to give them money. On the other hand, if they put up convincing shows, they can easily win sympathy.

They are Intelligent

It takes a lot of intelligence to convince the human brain to perceive reality in a manner that it would doubt in normal circumstances. Crafting an effective plan after observing a person for a short or long while is a tough task. However, deceivers are swift at decoding human behavior. They can predict the outcome of situations before they happen and plan accordingly. Intelligence is also required when dealing with the cognitive load which they carry. It helps them to overcome this limiting factor without leaking their plans and/or intentions.

They are Confident

Confidence is one of the most attractive and convincing human traits. Confidence is the ability to approach people and situations without fear or doubt. When someone comes up to us smiling and speaking fluently, we are more likely to listen to them. Conversely, if someone tries to talk to us, yet they are inaudible or shy, our attention and interest are lost. That said, a deceiver tries to be very confident when making their moves to minimize suspicion and improve their overall appearance. They seem to have satisfactory answers to everything. Confidence is very important to them because they also need to overcome their conscience, which might discourage them from taking advantage of others.

They are Eloquent

Liars are either born with eloquence, or they practice it. They are said to be smooth, natural performers. During an interaction, they take charge and make the moment as lively as possible. They speak without stammering or hesitating even when talking about false things. Deceivers come off as excellent listeners as they know people are attracted to those who give them an ear. When it is their turn to speak, even after some doubt is cast, their wordplay is powerful to the extent that it can make a lie to be acceptable. "Ers" and "Uhm" are never part of their vocabulary.

They are Keen

Unknown to us, we have an innate gift of detecting suspicion when we have done something wrong. For instance, if we lie about our ages, we watch out for clues which may hint that the other party is not taking the lie. Some clues might be raising their eyebrows, looking at us from head to toe or throwing a sarcastic statement which seeks to doubt. Similarly, deceivers are overly keen. They know how to read verbal cues and body language. This skill is used to evaluate their progress, know when to change a narrative, or abandon the mission in general.

They have a Sharp Memory

You have probably heard the saying that the disadvantage of lying is that you must force yourself to remember everything. One of the betrayers of deception is giving contradicting statements from what one had previously stated. A keen subject can detect a deceiver if they notice a conflicting narrative. To overcome this shortfall, deceivers have adapted by developing a sharp memory. If someone asks them about something they had said previously, they give the exact sentiments. This single trait alone makes it hard for them to blunder and very hard for outsiders to detect their fallacies.

They Speak Half-truths

The high intelligence that deceivers possess increases their prowess at misleading people. They understand that fabricating a lie from scratch is hard and is easier to be detected. Therefore, they resort to bending truths. A half-truth is more convincing as part of it can be verified. It also translates to less cognitive load since they only need to fabricate part of the story. For example, a retail store might announce a sale where they have slashed the prices of vegetables. While this might be true, they might as well be selling the vegetables cheaply since they are of inferior quality. To them, they have no remorse for selling bad groceries as long as they prevent losses at the expense of the customers.

They are Expressive

A deceiver is bound to be someone who can express an idea in a way such that the recipient has no room for questions or doubts. They are good with detailing and articulating issues because a narrative that has no loopholes is easier to adopt. The expressiveness is deployed at their first interaction with the target as a way to create a good first impression. First impressions influence the way we see others. As such, if they make it worthwhile at first interaction, they make the target easier to influence due to their good image.

False lovers are examples of expressive people. When asked why they love someone, they provide juicy reasons which convince their innocent others.

They are Rapid Thinkers

The other trait that is commonly seen in liars is the ability to think fast. This is especially true with the deceivers who hunt for victims in public or when they have limited time. They have to come up with effective plans in the shortest way possible before their subjects disappear or become suspicious. Similarly, they also display rapid thinking when they are cornered or forced to make impromptu explanations. Some of them are professionals in the art of deception that they can come up with the most convincing statements in a short while.

A good example of rapid thinking is deployed by salespeople. During their marketing sprees, they can meet with potential customers who ask all sorts of questions. For instance, a lady intending to purchase a watch might ask, "Is this one waterproof?" The salesperson, aiming at securing a deal, rushes to respond, "Yes, Madam. Not even air can get inside. Our bosses use these watches, and I'm only selling it to you because you are dressed like a boss!" Such trickery easily wins the trust of the client who might get home only to find the watch is the opposite of everything they were told.

They are Decent

There is a funny but unfair observation in psychology

that attractive people are more likely to be trusted than their average-looking counterparts. The deceiver of today comes off as a chivalrous gentleman or well-groomed lady. Humans are used to "bad" people possessing hard looks or being unfriendly. This is an outdated notion because deceivers have evolved into the charming people we meet online, the needy children we pity, the beautiful women we find with flat tires around the corner and the same people whose glowing faces we see the first thing in the morning. The deception begins with the creation of false trust.

They are Cold-blooded

Empathy is the innate feeling, which limits the extent to which we can get when interacting with others. If we place ourselves in their shoes and have a feel of what bad actions would have on them, we naturally react by not doing them or by making it up to them. Deceivers are a different breed. They do not experience any guilt or remorse when they harm someone. This is partly because they know emotional reactions can hinder their plans, and, in addition, because they are masters at suppressing their emotions. Their dark sides are exposed when they are caught or after they have achieved their objectives.

For example, a man might seduce a lady, pretending to love her. After some time, the lady gets pregnant, and the man abandons her since he did not genuinely love her, but used her for sex. He may ignore her advances henceforth and turn abusive in a way the lady would not have anticipated before the pregnancy. It is at this time that she sees his true colors; which are that of a psychopath.

Deceivers, as it is evident above, possess a lot of admirable traits. They package themselves in a manner that disarms suspicion while earning them instant trust. These traits make them very hard to detect. All the same, most of their characteristics are false, meaning they can drop them accidentally; exposing their malicious intents. It is important to consider that while a person might portray one or more of these characteristics, they do not automatically qualify as deceivers.

Areas of Our Lives where Deception Is Common

People deceive each other every day. Lying and cheating are acceptable human traits if they are controlled. However, just like everything else, if overdone, deception can ruin our interpersonal interactions and cause far much bigger problems in society.

Everywhere there are humans, deception must exist. That said, we shall list some of the areas in our lives where a deception is a common event.

Social Media

Social media is a virtual community that unites the entire world through internet connectivity. It allows people to create their preferred profiles and interact with the rest of the world using them. The aspect of social media, which makes it a commonplace for deception to occur is that a person can use false information to set up a profile. When this happens, the people in his or her circle think they know the real person when, in reality, they do not exist. False information such as incorrect age, wrong gender, inaccurate place of origin, race, profession, and much more is easily provided. Therefore, the people who interact with such a person are deceived into believing they are interacting with a genuine person.

The other way that social media can be deceiving is when people use engineered images and videos to create a better impression of themselves. They might attract other people with whom they eventually meet up beyond the virtual world. To the shock of many people who meet this way, they find that the people they meet are totally different from the ones they had seen online. Such interactions end up being disappointing, and one party feels cheated or taken advantage of.

Romantic Relationships

Deception thrives exponentially in romantic relationships because of the number of emotions invested in them. The high connectivity means that when one partner decides to deceive the other, they can do it easily without being detected. One of the most common forms of deception can happen when one partner talks their lover into initiating a romantic partnership, yet they are not genuinely in love with them. They might be pursuing hidden agendas such as sexual or financial benefits. Toxic lovers may even manipulate their partners just to play with their feelings.

Another occurrence that is not new in love bonds is cheating. This is the situation whereby one partner has extramarital affairs. They go out with third parties while keeping their loves in the false belief that they are faithful. In such circumstances, the partner who is being cheated upon is being deceived. Their trust has been won and used to gain an advantage over them such that they cannot realize that their lovers are sleeping with others.

Criminal Justice System

Deception in the criminal justice system begins with the interaction between law enforcers and suspects. When the suspects are arrested, they always try to convince the police that they are innocent to avoid the trips to the police stations. At this point, they may try to twist the truth to prove their innocence; which they sometimes succeed in doing. For example, an overspeeding driver might lie to a traffic officer that they were rushing to pick their wives or kids who have collapsed in the house. Owing to this high-risk situation, the officer might believe them and set them free.

The second level in the justice system where deception is a frequent visitor is during court sessions. Lawyers are the main culprits here. They are paid by criminals who know too well they are guilty of their crimes to try and save them from incarceration. Depending on the presentation of facts and countering the prosecution, hardcore criminals such as murderers and fraudsters might end up returning to society. In such instances, the lawyers are said to have deceived the prosecution and assisted a criminal in getting away with a crime.

On yet another level, criminals in jail understand that if they displayed reformed behavior, they could be paroled way before the end of their sentences. To achieve parole, they use disguise to create the impression of reformed prisoners. Some of them are lucky enough to fool the prison systems. Once out of jail, they can drop their fake personalities and return to lives of crime.

The Military

We have all heard stories of how armies in the two World Wars deployed an array of mind control tricks to get leverage over their opponents. One of the tactics we know of was the use of decoy tankers and planes to throw enemy troops off balance. An army would send a platoon of fake tankers and planes towards the enemy. When the enemy responded, the army would approach them from a different angle and ambush them. This amounted to the use of diversion to deceive their enemies.

Militaries are also the kings of camouflage. Everything from their backpacks to gear and vehicles, planes, and infrastructure are all made to blend in with the environment. Camouflage enables them to hide their presence when they do not need attention. In the World Wars, armies were known to cover their tankers and trucks with jungle-green canvas to conceal them from enemy planes. In this way, they played the absence trick on them.

E-commerce

Electronic markets are the most preferred shopping avenues on the planet as at today. People enjoy the comfort of making purchases online and having their goods delivered to their doorsteps. However, this efficiency also comes with a cost.

First, there is the risk of being defrauded. An online shop might pretend to be genuine and market itself online. When a customer makes a purchase, though, they take their money but fail to honor their side of the deal. Fraud is a form of deception. A scenario like this means the buyer trusted the vendor with their money, but the vendor was not genuine all along.

There is another emerging trend where online vendors are advertising items, but upon purchase, the clients realize they have been shortchanged. For instance, you might come across a lovely pair of gold-coated shoes going for an unbelievably low price. Upon ordering them, however, you have a pair of doll shoes delivered! Well, it is the very same pair that you saw online, only that they never said they were doll shoes. Camera angles and editing were used to make the impression that they were average human shoes.

Drug Abuse

Did you know that over 60% of all drug users were introduced by their acquaintances? Now you know! We can make an assumption that most of those influenced were asked to "take a puff," "just one jab," or "try one for the road" only to wake up one morning and find that they were regular smokers or drunkards. The influence of this type qualifies as deception because if the person did not consent to try them out but was seduced or coerced, it was against their will. Concisely, they were cheated into trying them out, and that ended up as being the start of a never-ending road to dependency.

The Media

The media is one of the biggest influencers in the world. Under this umbrella term, we have music, advertisements, films, papers, magazines, and news. The list is endless. Since we depend on information from the media to plan our lives, we subconsciously become their puppets.

If we look at the issue of fake news, they can cause panic, misinform the masses, or cause civil unrest such as clashes. Unfortunately for us, we tend to blindly absorb everything we are fed by news sources. The issue of fake news took headlines after the 2016 election of US President Donald Trump. Some newspapers claimed he would deport all non-

Americans while some claimed his supporters were attacking non-Whites. This led to protests and minor skirmishes in some major states like New York, Oakland, Seattle, Philadelphia, and Chicago. Years after his election, the news came to pass as false. The media had deceived the Americans.

The deceptive influence of music cannot be overlooked. In recent times, it has been observed that the lifestyles displayed by musicians can be misleading to some audiences. Young people, who are the most affected, believe everything they see in the videos is true. They try to live like the musicians and when they fail, negative cognitive effects such as low self-esteem and depression kick in. As such, we can quantify some music at potential deceiving.

Communication

Last but not least, we have communication in terms of interpersonal relationships. Unpleasant conversations like gossiping and shaming are composed of false information about other people. Deceivers can use badmouthing to talk foul about others with the aim of painting them in a bad light. If the receivers of false information believe in it, the victim of the gossip or shaming gains a negative but false reputation; making it be deception. Deception of this kind makes use of lies and diversion to achieve its mandate.

Now that we have covered the traits that a manipulative individual seeks and their reasons, let's review how you can spot manipulation to avoid becoming their next victim. As you can see, a manipulator excels in applying psychological techniques that are meant to build relationships, only with a sinister twist, to achieve their goals. It is important to be aware of their subtle tricks and there a few more overt aggressive signals that you want to be on the lookout for. To protect yourself from becoming a puppet, you will have to pay attention to these signs that are the earmarks of a manipulative individual.

Psychology Tricks Used for Persuasion

When you are with someone, pay attention to their conversation habits. If most of their conversation is based around words that are mainly focused on their own life, their own experiences and they do not ask questions about you or your interests, then they are potentially manipulative and self-centered. These individuals always talk about themselves, brag a lot, making sure to keep the topic on their life, their "accomplishments", on what they are doing and how they are feeling. This is a power play for getting you to completely focus your attention on them. This is essentially baiting the hook, they want to be sure you are thinking about them and their situation, not yourself and your needs when they make the "ask".

The manipulative individual can be charismatic, charming and even flattering, which disarms the unknowing victim. When the off chance occurs and they do ask how you are, they do not listen to your answer. They will smile convincingly, even leaning in to appear interested, but it becomes evident they were not listening when they are unable to recall the details of your response. They will often blow past anything you say moving on to other topics or direct the conversation back to themselves. This is telling of their insecurity and insincerity.

They pretend to be interested in what you are saying to them without contributing to the conversation. They will stand with their arms akimbo, gesturing towards you with an open hand, they will nod at what you are saying to feign agreement. This nodding and open hand is a physical cue that there is a request coming. The core goal in their mind is to find a way to slip in what they want. They will look you up and down or hold eye contact for an unusually long period as a method of subconsciously controlling you. They will place themselves within close quarters to you because body proximity tends to influence others, using body language coupled with the "mirroring" technique is a sure-fire method of reeling a victim into their game.

A manipulative person is someone that wants something from you. You will find them presenting themselves in a pleasing fashion, being overly complimentary in conversation and always telling you what you want to hear. They always seem outrageously excited to see you or be around you. They will be charismatic, charming and will use flattery knowing that buttering you up and sweet-talking you will gain them favor in your eyes. They are softening you up to ask you for a favor or pitch you an idea.

They will often couple asking for a favor with the

promise to return the favor. They will suggest their ideas to you while expressing there is an emotional benefit to you by fulfilling their request. When they finally make their desired goal known they use a "slick salesman" type of psychology by implying that, if you do their bidding, there will be some sort of value or reward in it for you. If you listen to what they are saying you will realize that they are making requests and following them with statements that are meant to convince you. The statements will usually be designed to convince you that helping them will be a good idea for you or improve your situation somehow. It is a good idea to evaluate their proposition to determine if you both will benefit from, or if this is just the manipulator's sly way to get your cooperation.

A manipulative person will be very kind and generous at first and say nice things about you, everyone wants to be approved of. The manipulator knows this and will use that in their favor. The person who is seeking manipulate will do so with good deeds. They will do something that appears nice and generous, but only if they stand to gain attention and a good reputation from it. Remember that manipulation can be hidden behind kind gestures, but their acts of generosity and gifts are bribes to make them look good in front of other people. These actions are usually coupled with an outward display. You will notice they behave differently when they are alone with you and no one is watching. They may amplify this "good deed" psychological manipulation technique with guilt. This person will never let you forget what they did, they will bring it up, reminding you and will continue to drain you in repayment for the one or two times they did something for you. This creates a rinse-repeat cycle of manipulation by continuously wanting repayment for obsolete or past behaviors, rather than focusing on the current dynamics of your relationship.

The manipulator will exaggerate and lie to get what they want. They will repeat the same stories over and over, with details varying each time but the main subject is always them. They will tell stories that are flattering to themselves, put them in a good light or are filled with false self-praise. They will tell complicated stories of being victimized that are filled with "poor me" rhetoric to gain sympathy from you. They will often say that they are ill or hurt to avoid responsibility. These manipulative and dysfunctional people do not communicate directly usually resorting to falsehoods, lies and elaborate stories that will pull on your emotions and compel your help, gain attention and even do their work for them, which is their desired goal.

The manipulator has another psychological tool that they employ to avoid working, praise. They will praise you for the kindness you possess so they can influence you to do what they want, and they are playing upon your good qualities. They will tell you how "nice" and "helpful" you are, then ask for something, knowing now that they have complimented your charitable helpful nature you are likely to do what they ask. They will commend you for having a skill or ability, with the underlying goal being they want you to live up to this talent. This is so they can get something out of you. They will say things like "You know you are a great writer. Can you help me draft my speech?" or "You are so good with people. I am putting you in charge of the dinner party, you'll do a better job." They make a flattering statement placing the thought in your head that you are "better" at something they are, then switch quickly to asking you do them a favor or volunteering you to fulfill a task you never asked for or that was their responsibility, to begin with. With these bait and switch techniques, the idea is to give you high praise regarding your skill at something, encourage your self-confidence, and then redirect the conversation toward asking you to do something they just do not want to do.

You might also be manipulated by someone through them leaning on your helpful nature. The manipulator will take advantage of you by asking for your "help" with something they do not want to do. The manipulative individual knows that people love to help others and teach others about something they possess knowledge in, they will use this to their benefit. You will also find the manipulator pretend to be "less than" in some particular task, saying that they are "not good" at something or that they just "do not know how" to do it, relying on you to do it for them. This type of manipulation can prove to be equally undermining as they may not admit to your helping them and many times will even take credit for a "job well done" by you.

A manipulative person will pressure you into deciding right away, not permitting you time to review your schedule or your feelings when responding to a request or appeal. They will give the matter a false sense of urgency, they will crowd your space not permitting you time to yourself to think about their actions and they expect you to immediately decide or satisfy their need. They do not ever question their actions and may have a delusional belief that they are correct to pressure you. They think they are the only one who knows what to do and may even reason to themselves that you should see that they are right. The only goal they have is to get you to do what they want, and they will play upon your emotions to achieve this end. The only goal they have is to get you to do what they want and will often make you feel guilty if you do not.

Notice that a manipulative individual will not take "no" for an answer to any request or demand they make. They will continue to belabor the point until you give in to their demands They play upon your feelings through shame, guilt, and obligation. This is especially true if they are a partner, family member or friend. They may say things like "I helped you when you needed it " using your shared bond or history to make you feel the weight of obligation. They may attempt to pressure you by questioning your loyalty to them with statements like "How can you tell me 'no', you're my sister?" or "If you loved me, you would do this for me. " They will resort to enforcing relationship history to supplant your decision "We have been friends for such a long time I think you would want to help me with this." They will cry, wheedle and sometimes become loud or aggressive if you tell them you are unable or unwilling to do what they want. An aggressive manipulator will often make their demands with loud demonstrations in public, forcing you to give in to their wants just to avoid embarrassment.

A passive-aggressive manipulator will "pout" like a child when you do not give in to their desires. They will eye-ball you while giving you the silent treatment and if you attempt to approach them regarding their behavior, they will often say they are "not mad" or just ignore you altogether. They will resort to "pay-back" tactics when you do not give in such as failing to do something they had promised to or letting you down in some fashion as a method of retribution. This type of manipulative individual will pull the "disappearing act" or "ghost" you which is another one of their top psychological punishments if you do not give in to them. They will break or fail to show up for plans, do not respond to your calls and ignore your messages as a way of making you suffer for not doing their bidding.

This type of manipulative person will also employ gas-lighting as a method of getting you back if you do not comply with their demands. You will find them making back-handed comments such as "That was a really great meal, too bad you don't always like that." or "I think it would be a great idea for you to go for that promotion, if you were more skilled at Marketing you would definitely get it." They will infer support while slyly inserting a statement or comment that is meant to insult you or attack your self-confidence. They will make fun of you and ridicule you and when confronted they will say they are "joking" or that you are being too "sensitive".

There is a dark side to gaslighting that can really push an insecure person into anxiety, depression or neurotic paranoia. This is when the manipulator will tell you something that really hurts or insults you to get back at you for not doing what they wanted. Then when confronted they say things like "I never said that. You're crazy." or "You are misinterpreting what I said, why would I say that to you?" This gas-lighting can extend to behaviors and actions as well with the manipulative person lying about their actions or telling the victim that they are not recalling the incident clearly and often will supply a completely fabricated version of the event. These aggressive attacks are designed to bully you into giving them what they want so you can avoid their punishment in the future.

Be aware, if you find yourself saying things like "I don't want to upset them." or "I will never hear the end of it." when contemplating saying "no" to someone or not responding to their request then you are probably being manipulated. Gas-lighting is one method of control, insults bring your self-esteem down making you easier to manipulate, but there are many subtle phrases that you will hear from someone that is trying to influence you into meeting their demands.

Phrases Manipulative People Use

We have reviewed the methods of psychological influence that employ phrasing to encourage others to see our point of view. Those methods of communicating that make others feel comfortable with us, like the "similarity" strategy, which can quickly bond us to others making them feel connected with us. But the manipulator will also use subliminal phrases that negatively influence us eliciting shame, guilt and sometimes even fear to force our hand and making us give in to their demands.

Many manipulative individuals will employ the dependency technique to psychologically influence others into doing what they want. This is the person who always seems to be in crisis or need of a helping hand. We explored this earlier when looking at the Dependent Personality Disorder, and it is not surprising to see this can be a manipulative technique as well. The phrases that are associated with dependence manipulation are designed to make you feel guilt or shame if you do not do what the manipulator wants.

The manipulative person will use emotional circumstances to make you feel guilty. They will ask you for help, make a request or demand that you be there for them in some circumstance and when you are unable or unwilling to meet their needs they will resort to guilt-inducing statements. They will use phrases like "If you don't do (request), I can't do this",

"You don't care about me", "I would do this for you" or "If you don't (request) then I have no one else to help me." The main theme of these statements is that they make you feel responsible. The subliminal point the manipulator is making here is that they are dependent upon you meeting their request for things to go well for them. They want you to know that if you do not comply with their demand it will somehow be your fault that things do not work out for them. This type of manipulation is supposed to make you feel guilty because they are completely dependent upon you. They pretend to be weak and powerless, enforcing the idea that you must not let them down.

When you give in to this type of manipulative individual, they will often have you overextend yourself or go out of your way for them no matter how inconvenient it is for you. If you do not give in to their unreasonable demands, they will never let you off the hook. This person does not see that you have a life or might not be comfortable with their requests, they cannot accept that you just might not want to do what they want. Much like a petulant child, they will continue to bring up how you "Let them down" or "Were not there for (them)." The manipulator will use this as ammunition in future situations. They will remind you of your "failure to be there" for them in one situation using that instance to guilt-trip you into giving in to them later regarding something else. They will often replay these same "let down" statements repeatedly, leveraging the guilt, no matter how many times you meet their demands afterward.

Many of these manipulative techniques that are re-used will often lead you to feel less-than and insecure, which will fuel the manipulator's tactical strategy of getting you to become co-dependent upon them. The manipulative person will use absolute terms combined with gaslighting to push your emotions an obtain what they want. They will remind you that you failed in one respect or another in their opinion saying statements like "You ALWAYS do this to me" or "You are NEVER there for me" these absolute terms are meant to convey their dependence on your support and make you feel shame for the perceived offense when you do not give in to their manipulation.

Another technique that the manipulator uses is the blame game. This is a broader play upon their philosophy that you are responsible for their actions and the circumstances in their lives. They will blast you with blame for something they did with comments like "Look what you made me do" or "If you weren't always in the way I wouldn't have dropped this." They will make you responsible for how events they are involved in turn out saying something like "If you had been there this would have gone a completely different" or "This wouldn't have happened if you had helped me." This type of manipulation is very arbitrary and will be thrown at you no matter what the real circumstance is. This is the blame game technique that many who are hard-wired for manipulation are apt to display.

They will often turn a situation around with statements like "I did do (that), but only because you did (this)" twisting it back on you or someone else, "If they did not do (that), I wouldn't have had to" indicating their actions are appropriate responses to the actions of someone else. The manipulator does not ever take responsibility for their own actions or the circumstances they are involved in. They believe that everything that goes wrong is the fault of someone else.

How to Tell if Someone is Lying to You

One of the manipulator's best weapons for deflecting responsibility is lying. The manipulator will flat out lie to avoid taking responsibility for their actions or any circumstance they have created. They will lie about things they have said to you, the things they have said to other people about you and will even lie to themselves. This type of individual has such a large capacity for denial that they will sway the opinion of others with their fabrications and even come to believe their own excuses after repeating them so often.

But how can you tell if a manipulator is lying to you? There are a few clear signs that you are being lied to, especially when someone is trying to manipulate you. You can start with their vehement use of absolute words such as "I would NEVER do that", or "I SWEAR" when they are denying something. They generally will accompany these types of statements with feigned indignation, but you will notice that there is no honesty in their eyes, so watch for this micro-expression. If they are lying to you, they will not blink. The manipulator will look you in the eye and when they lie their eyes will not blink and then right after they complete the lie you will notice they blink rapidly several times. This is due to their nervousness in their knowledge that they have just lied to you.

Other physical signs that will let you know that someone is being untruthful with you are small body movements and excessive fidgeting. A good portion of the conversation especially when lying they cannot look you in the eye. You will see them looking down and looking away when they speak to you, especially if giving you an explanation or falsely promising something. They will blink slowly and then pull their head back or tilt it to the side before responding to avoid looking you in the face. They may touch their face, or their ears pointing to evasiveness.

When confronted they will respond with an answer that is vague like "I don't know", and "I don't remember". They may respond with very detailed and elaborate stories, or they may give you an answer that when pressed again the response changes or is inconsistent. Look for simulated facial expressions such as a smile that does not reach their eyes or crying that does not produce tears. Look for the crease between their eyes and pay attention to their jawline muscle, because if it tenses this indicates they're under stress. Look for small ticks or twitching while you are speaking to them or nervous laughing. They pull away, exhibit very controlled and limited body movement. They might cross their arms, or their legs, zip up their jacket or button their sweater. Ask an unrelated and unexpected question, then repeat the same statement or the same question you started with. Notice if their response changes. Ask them to repeat their story in reverse. When a person is lying, they cannot repeat the same contrived story backward.

Another way to spot a lie is if the person gets angry with you when their response is fraught with hostility it is a good sign, they are not telling the truth. They may just respond in an obnoxious tone. If you are dealing with a very manipulative person who is lying to you, they will resent that they are being confronted by anyone. They may have an indignant outburst of anger, be aware this may be a very loud and demonstrative outburst, so be cautious when you are dealing with someone like this. When confronted with their lies they may react with completely disproportionate anger. You may be asking them something simple like "Did you see my laptop?" and find them responding in a loud voice and aggressive manner, railing at you that they are "Not a thief! How dare you assume that I would take it! I don't know where your stupid laptop is!" Look for this steam roller technique as it is the manipulators' way of bullying you into believing them.

Signs Someone is Using Psychology to Manipulate You

It is important to realize that the manipulative individual will use any means necessary to get you to fill their need for attention, gain control and do their bidding. This type of individual thrives off controlling another person and will use their body language and manipulative wording to obtain the control they are seeking. There a few combined actions and phrases that will let you know when someone is using psychology to manipulate you. Once you have learned the combination of persuasion methods they employ, you will be less likely to fall into their trap.

There are many reasons that someone will try to persuade you, like when they are suggesting to you or requesting your help with something. When the individual is sincere there is an open dialogue. Their honesty will be expressed in their facial expressions and that sincerity will reach their eyes. Possessing relaxed body language and facing you directly, they will wait patiently for your response.

The opposite is true when you are being manipulated by someone who only wants you to comply with their desires. The manipulative person will demand that you give them an immediate response when they ask you to do something or when they request anything from you. Their body language will be tense while feigning altruism and their smiles will not reach their eyes. They will place their bodies in very close proximity and engage in prolonged eye contact, especially when providing a directive or making uncomfortable demands. The combination of these subliminal signals is meant specifically to intimidate and pressure you.

Flattery is another method that a manipulative person will use to persuade you to do their bidding. The individual that uses this method to encourage another to give in to them will often combine it with warm gesturing and a lot of eye contact. This person will "mirror" you and use the "similarity" strategy. This person will engage in polite banter asking how things are with you. They appear to listen intently to your conversation leaning in and looking you in the eye. They will let the conversation go on and when presented with the right opening, will almost too quickly reply with "I feel the same way" or " I completely understand how you feel", they will be quick to make the sympathetic identification with you to gain your favor. Then when the moment is ripe they will slip in "By the way, I was wondering if" or "You know that reminds me, I have been meaning to ask you" You will be able to spot their insincerity when their request or favor immediately follows their exclaiming how they feel the same way as you. This is a unique method of psychological manipulation and may take a while to pick up on because you will have been engaged in conversation with them for a few minutes before they will make their true intentions known. A big key to spotting this particular method of psychological manipulation is that this person will seem almost too happy to see you when approaching you as if it has been years since they have seen you and you are the only person in the world. This over-excited greeting pattern is designed to make you feel special and warm you up to them immediately.

Another method of manipulation is displayed by anger. They may begin by asking you to do something for them but more often, than not they just tell you using words like "I want you to" or "you had better do this." This is usually characterized by intense demands, aggressively repeating the demand or request and implying that there will be a negative result if you do not give in. This person will yell at you and sometimes become physically agitated. You will see their neck muscles straining and their face contorting in an ugly fashion as they tell you what they expect you to do for them. This person will not be attempting to identify with or flatter your abilities hoping to gain your favor. This person will be domineering, loud and obnoxious, basically just telling you what to do. This direct bullying tactic is very evident and if you are being treated in this fashion you should never engage and definitely, do not give in to the demands of this manipulative individual. Avoid this confrontation and remove yourself from their presence swiftly.

The exact opposite of the aggressive manipulator is the needy request. This type of manipulation is displayed in the manner of hopelessly needing your help and is often accompanied by the sad face, big-eyed plea or begging to get your help with something. They will often display depressed body language with slumped shoulders and a drooping head. They will ask you for your help in an almost whining voice indicating they are desperate for your help. This person then uses the psychological method of imploring you repeatedly to help them, to get you to do what they are asking. They say things like " Please" and " I really need your help with this" but the red flag that this is a manipulation tactic is once you give in, they are suddenly fine. You will notice their body language abruptly shift and they will perk up. This will make you feel good because they are no longer sad, and they are because you have given in to their demand. This person will use this method repeatedly once they find it has the desired result, so watch for it.

The last method is as we must discuss is gas-lighting. This person will have a history of employing demeaning and insulting comments that degrade you and destroy your self-confidence. They will say rude and unacceptable things to you and then say they are "only joking" and that you are "too sensitive." This is a method they will use on you repeatedly and then they will follow with statements like "C'mon you know I'm only kidding, I love you" or "Jeez, it's just a joke! You're my best friend we joke with each other all the time." The psychological technique to notice here is that by tearing you down they are building themselves up and making them appear somehow superior in your eyes. This method is to encourage you to give your power to them. If they are the "alpha" in the relationship you will naturally do their bidding in every situation and not even question it. They know this and it is a method of manipulation they have used successfully all their lives.

You will notice this person speak the same way to everyone and never admits to it. This is the person that will say " I never said that" or " That is now how I said it" and then conveniently change their statements around. This is the person that in a tense situation or disagreement will remain calm and cool when you get upset at their obvious lying. They may even laugh at you when you point out they are not recalling their statements or actions correctly. They will say things like "You are crazy" thereby making it appear you are out of control. They often combine this with the silent treatment telling you they will not speak with you until you "have pulled yourself together." This is a major psychology play after they have insulted you, offended you or wronged you in some fashion and is often combined with statements like "you are blowing this way out of proportion" or "you are overreacting." This is said to undermine you and make you doubt your memory of the entire event or conversation. This is a sinister method that once used on you successfully, may even be amped-up with the manipulator telling you an entirely different version of the events, expecting you to believe their version because your memory is inaccurate. Gaslighting becomes a very common and powerful psychological control tool when you are in a co-dependent relationship with a manipulative individual.

Power Persuasion Techniques Used in Manipulation

Unfortunately, when you are dealing with someone on a personal or professional level that is manipulative their psychological methods of persuasion are almost always being used to their advantage in every situation. These persuasion techniques become second nature to the manipulative individual and make them comes across as a powerful person when they are using them. These skills of persuasion have been finely honed with their success demonstrated repeatedly to the manipulator. We must keep in mind; this individual may not even know that they are using these methods of communication to manipulate you. The use of these techniques is instinctive because they have given the manipulator an edge in their social communication and obtained for them all their goals. Just like an athlete that has built up his muscles to achieve the win, the manipulative individual has become very skilled in using these power persuasion techniques to achieve their aim. We are going to look at a few of these power persuasion techniques and why they work with the goal being that you will be able to spot and put a stop to this controlling behavior.

The first technique that a manipulative individual will employ is avoidance. This is when you find you are asking a question and they reply with a question, or when you are speaking to them about something, they will switch the topic over to you. Many times, they will redirect your thoughts, they will flip questions back on you or start asking you an unrelated question. They will point out something you did instead of responding to you or dealing with the subject you are addressing. They always say the right thing, truthful or not to end the line of questioning pointed at them They will accuse you of behaviors that are aimed at making them feel bad when you attempt to make it clear that they have done or said something that has made you upset or has you concerned. It is not beneath them to say things like "You are a liar". They will flat out deny their actions and fight for the last word every time, just to win their point.

The cold manipulator who is seeking control over a sensitive individual will say things like "You are selfish", "You don't care about me", You are so cruel" or "You are so cold and uncaring" to upset your emotional balance and make you feel guilty. You will often be accused of doing the very thing that they did by making accusations like "Well you did this and you know how much that hurts me" the point will be to make you see they are being treated worse and distract your attention from the calculated way they have behaved. They will augment these statements as you move further into conflict by indicating to you that you could not possibly understand how much worse you made them feel rather than admitting what they have done to you. This avoidance of responsibility is a common practice for the manipulator as they are never at fault in their own eyes.

They use these attacks on your character knowing that you will relent with your direction of thought or stop questioning them. They will say things that paint you as a hurtful and heartless person so you will focus on showing them that you have the opposite positive qualities. They also use this weapon combined with guilt to keep you locked in a dysfunctional cycle of communication. By flipping boundaries around and accusing you of being selfish, unsupportive or cold, the manipulator will achieve their goal and have you scurrying to meet their needs.

They will use your sensitivity and breed insecurity in you to destroy your self-confidence and gain a foothold in your life. They want to be the only person that you will trust and turn to and they want to be the center of attention in every instance. They do this by presenting themselves as your confident while feeding you information that is offensive, destructive and designed to hurt you. They will often instigate disharmony by telling you something unkind that someone "allegedly" said about you under the guise of caring about your feelings, like "I'm sorry, I shouldn't tell you this, but so and so said " then drop a nasty or insulting comment another has said. Then they will follow it up with reassurance such as "don't worry, I have your back, I know you are not like that." seeking to divide you from others.

Another power persuasion technique used by the manipulator to undermine your self-confidence is their use of left-handed remarks. They will ask you a question like "I would never wear something so garish, but it looks good on you." or " Have you lost weight? You were really 'porking-out' there for a while." or highlight that "you look better than the last time" they saw you, inferring you looked ragged or worn prior. They will point out your vulnerabilities or something they know you feel insecure about and then follow that up with a statement affirming how much they like or care about you.

Another method they will use in pushing their agenda is forcing you into actions or activities that you may not want to do by implying it is for "your best interest" or "it will be good for you". They will use statements like "You know I wouldn't steer you wrong" or needle you with questions like "Don't you trust me?" This sort of power persuasion technique can be used perfectly to hold you back from trying new things or believing in yourself. When combined with implied constructive criticism it is very persuasive, the manipulator will say things like "I only want what is best for you" or "You know I'm always looking out for you" implying that they are holding you back or checking your self-confidence as a way of protecting you.

The thing to keep in mind with these power persuasion techniques is that they are designed to undermine you, make you feel uncomfortable and cut you off from supportive friends and family. The manipulative individual has the aim of becoming the only person you can "count' on so they can have that as a bargaining tool in the future to get you to do what they want. One of the key goals of the manipulator is that they want you to replay the hurtful things they say to you in your head. This will enable them to exert continued control over you because you will want to prove yourself to them.

The manipulator is seeking to get a response out of you, preferably they want you to defend yourself. The manipulator thrives off drama, discord, and dysfunction. This heightened emotional state that they place you in fuels their desire for complete focus. The result is that you are doing two things: one, you are completely fixated on them while neglecting yourself and two, when you are defending yourself you are in a state of emotional fatigue with the round and round arguments. This gives them leverage in every situation as they know eventually you will give up completely and they will "win" the battle. They will feed off your sense of being overwhelmed, your anxiety and your frustration. They will use these emotions to further convince you that you are not supportive enough or compassionate.

This will invariably lead you to display the opposite to the manipulator, giving in to their demands, no matter how outlandish they are or how inconvenient to you. The main powerful persuasion strategy being applied here is our universal need to be liked and held in esteem by others. People want to be known as helpful, kind and generous. They want to be considered good neighbors, reliable colleagues, and supportive friends to those they care about.

CONCLUSION

Finally, I am glad you made it to the end of this book. By now you would have mapped out a plan with the techniques provided in this book on how to manipulate, influence, persuade, and change people's minds. We all have different ways of doing and saying things and knowing the right way to do them will help you win when people are involved. This book contains secret techniques and step-by-step methods in which you can trigger people's emotions and be in charge. I have written this book in a very simple and easy manner so that a beginner and an expert can equally benefit from it.

Manipulation, persuasion, naked influence, and the art of reading people's mind are concepts that will aid you in getting the end result you want to see. They all have some basic differences between them, but the similarity between them is that they are all a form of human communication. As humans, we are easily changed by what we see and listen to each day. These three concepts all involve getting another person or people to do what you want. In this book, I talked about their meaning, some modern-day examples of how they are used, and techniques you can use to successfully put them in good use.

Also, I want to congratulate you for showing an interest in a subject like this. Only a few people will want to understand the social skills involved in manipulating, persuading and influencing others. Most people are interested in learning other social skills but neglecting these arts that I have talked about. Manipulation, influencing, and persuasion manifests wherever we go: starting with spouses that are attempting to change the unpleasant behavior of their partner to a mother that is trying to convince her child to eat broccoli. It is used by teachers who try to shape their student's mind to choose the best path of their career; leaders that motivate their followers to get involved in noble causes; and people who help others overcome hurdles, solve their problems, accept challenges, and rise above the struggles. These people are all using the art of manipulation, influence, and persuasion. This shows influence moving from one point to another in an ethical way. Remember don't hurt others in the process of using it. Always use these techniques out of respect for the other person.

Again, I want to use this opportunity to say thank you for staying with me throughout the book. I know it's a challenging one but at the same time, you will agree with me that it is exciting. I believe you have gained a lot and will be using the techniques shared in this book carefully to get what you want. Reading this book won't be enough, you have to be practical with these techniques and have a genuine will to carry them out effectively.

www.ingramcontent.com/pod-product-compliance
Lightning Source LLC
Chambersburg PA
CBHW050726030426
42336CB00012B/1433